SLAYING ATLANTA

Curated by Leigh M. Clark

Aurora Corialis Publishing

Pittsburgh, PA

SLAYING ATLANTA

Printed in the United States of America

Edited by: Renee Picard, Aurora Corialis Publishing

Cover Design: Leigh M. Clark

Paperback ISBN: 978-1-958481-38-7

Ebook ISBN: 978-1-958481-39-4

OTHER COLLECTIVES BY LEIGH M. CLARK

Slaying Southwest Florida

Slaying Tampa Bay

Slaying Nashville

Slaying Sarasota

Slaying Chicago

The Dream is in Your Hands

The Dream is in Your Hands: She Can Do It

Living Kindly: Bold Conversations About the Power of

Kindness

Table of Contents

Introduction

The Magic of Atlanta and the Women Who Slay It

Leigh M. Clark

Atlanta, Ga., is a city that exudes vibrancy, resilience, and a relentless spirit of innovation. Known as the "City in a Forest," Atlanta blends a rich history with a modern, bustling atmosphere that draws people from all walks of life. From its world-renowned music scene to its cutting-edge cuisine and diverse neighborhoods, Atlanta is a place where dreams are both born and realized. But what truly sets this city apart is the women who drive its dynamism. These women are the entrepreneurs, creators, and leaders who embody the soul of Atlanta—a blend of tenacity and grace that fuels the city's ever-evolving narrative. They are the faces behind *Slaying Atlanta*, the women whose stories are intertwined with the growth and spirit of this remarkable city. They are women to watch, admire, and learn from, and they have authored the pages of the book you now hold in your hands.

My connection with Atlanta deepened in the summer of 2015, during a special project for a large national deals website I worked for at the time. That summer, I, along with about ten colleagues, spent the entire season exploring every corner of Atlanta—from the upscale streets of Buckhead to the historic charm of Vinings and the bustling energy of Smyrna. Each day brought a new adventure as we immersed ourselves in the city's diverse neighborhoods, each with its own unique character, style, and rhythm.

Atlanta is not a city you can describe in broad strokes; it's a mosaic of experiences and cultures, a place where every neighborhood tells a different story. In Buckhead, we marveled at the towering glass skyscrapers and luxury boutiques, a stark contrast to the quiet, tree-lined streets of Vinings, where history seemed to seep from every brick and stone. Smyrna, on the other hand, buzzed with a sense of community, a place where old and new Atlanta came together in a harmonious blend.

But what struck me most during that summer was not just the diversity of the city itself, but the way it pulsed with life—with art, music, and cuisine that reflected the rich tapestry of cultures that call Atlanta home. Every corner of the city felt like a celebration of creativity, from the murals that adorned the walls of downtown buildings to the soulful sounds that spilled out from local bars and restaurants. And through it all, it was the women of Atlanta who stood out—strong, innovative, and unafraid to push boundaries.

The Women of *Slaying Atlanta*: Visionaries, Innovators, and Leaders

Slaying Atlanta is more than just a phrase—it's a movement of women who are making waves in the city and beyond. These women are entrepreneurs, artists, community leaders, and rising stars, each embodying the spirit of Atlanta with their boldness, creativity, and determination. They are shaping the future of Atlanta, and their influence is felt far beyond the city limits.

Take, for example, Brittney Q. Hill who has not only achieved fame in the entertainment industry, she's also used her platform to inspire others to live in faith and gratitude. Her show *Faith and Fame TV* leads and inspires others to become their highest selves and to love one another. She is just one of the many women featured in this anthology who embody the spirit of Atlanta—resilient, creative, and unapologetically ambitious.

Then there's Serena Sacks-Mandel, a woman who has served as a C-level executive at one of the most globally known tech companies, and has made significant impacts in the philanthropy space. Her journey has been marked by challenges, but also by the impact she's made—changing the narrative in a field traditionally dominated by men. Serena is another example of how the women of *Slaying Atlanta* are redefining success in the city, using their talents to not only advance their own careers but to lift others as well.

These women, and so many others like them in this book, are setting the standard for what it means to succeed in Atlanta. They are the ones to follow, to admire, and to learn from. They have authored the pages of this book, sharing their stories of triumph and challenge. Their journeys are a testament to the fact that Atlanta is not just a city of opportunity, but a city where those opportunities can be seized and transformed into lasting success.

Atlanta's Growth and the Role of Women

Atlanta's population has been steadily growing, reflecting its status as a major cultural and economic hub in the Southeast. With a population exceeding 500,000 within the city limits and over six million in the metropolitan area, Atlanta has become a melting pot of cultures, industries, and ideas. Women make up just over 50 percent of this population, and their influence is felt in every sector—from business and education to arts and technology. The women featured in *Slaying Atlanta* are at the forefront of this growth, leading the charge in shaping Atlanta's future and ensuring that the city remains a place where everyone has the opportunity to succeed.

As Atlanta continues to evolve, so too does its cultural landscape. The city's rich history is complemented by its forward-thinking approach to development, making it a place where tradition and innovation coexist harmoniously. This blend is evident in the city's neighborhoods, each one offering a different slice of Atlanta's identity. Whether it's the historic charm of Grant Park, the modern hustle of Midtown, or the eclectic vibe of Little Five Points, Atlanta is a city that embraces its past while always looking toward the future.

The Spirit of Atlanta: A Personal Connection

Reflecting on that summer of 2015, I'm reminded of how deeply Atlanta resonated with me. It wasn't just the neighborhoods or the culture that left an impression—it was the people. Every interaction felt like a window into the soul of the city, revealing a community that is as diverse as it is united in its passion for growth and innovation. That summer, I felt a connection to Atlanta that has stayed with me, a sense of belonging in a city that thrives on creativity and ambition.

One evening, after a particularly long day of exploring, a few colleagues and I found ourselves at a local jazz club in the heart of Midtown. As the smooth, soulful sounds filled the room, I realized that this was Atlanta—a city where music, culture, and community come together to create something truly special. It's a city that welcomes you with open arms, where every street and every neighborhood has a story to tell. And at the heart of those stories are the women who make Atlanta what it is—dynamic, resilient, and endlessly inspiring.

A City of Vision and the Women Who Bring It to Life

In the end, it's the people who make Atlanta special—the vibrant, unique individuals who bring the city to life, the women who drive its success, and the dreamers who fill its streets with hope and ambition. Each visit to Atlanta reminds me of the city's beauty, its potential, and the power of community to shape our lives in meaningful ways. And at the heart of it all are the women of *Slaying Atlanta*, who are not only a part of the city's past and present but are instrumental in shaping its future.

The women of *Slaying Atlanta* have authored the pages of this book, sharing their stories of vision, innovation, and leadership. They are the heartbeat of Atlanta, and they are the reason this city continues to thrive. Their journeys are a testament to the fact that Atlanta is not just a city of dreams but a city where those dreams can be realized through hard work, determination, and a commitment to excellence.

May Dessert Be With You

Glynnis and Katha Waters

Sisters Glynnis and Katha began CEG over ten years ago in the Buckhead community after being inspired by Parisian artistry and bakeries during a trip to Paris.

These sisters believe community is family, and love having their treats integrated into the stories and celebrations of their clients. They blend traditional Southern heritage recipes, inspiration from travel, and classic French techniques to create elevated treats. All CEG goods are made with fresh, seasonal, natural, and local ingredients. Pure vanilla, shell eggs, European butter, and fresh fruits are the hallmark of CEG treats. All goods are baked in small batches to maintain optimal freshness. CEG

Bakery values quality in food and service, and their goal is to create an emotional experience through their food.

For the Waters sisters, baking and cooking have been long-standing family traditions since the age of five. In addition to home training, Glynnis and Katha trained and graduated from Le Cordon Bleu in patisserie and boulangerie. CEG has an array of clients from corporate, to private catering and weddings in addition to the daily baked and custom items in the shop. They have participated in *Dessert Wars*, the Big Game VIP experience, and have been featured in various series, including AE's *Secret Sauce* and recently Peachtree TV's *The Black Friday Report*.

Website: CEGbakery.com
Pastry Post (Instagram): CEG_bakery_official

———

CEG Bakery's journey didn't begin 10 years ago. In fact, it began over 40 years ago in our mother's kitchen, which created our love of cooking. Like many families, love, food, tradition, and faith are intertwined experiences for us. Our food reflects our spirituality; we want people to feel the love and hospitality as you enjoy it, this is deeply rooted in CEG's foundational principles. That magical feeling we get when we prepare a meal for our family and watch as the food is enjoyed, never goes away. We hope to create the same feelings and memories we grew up with, for our customers and their families. By preparing new and personalized experiences through our desserts, we have been able to help our clients celebrate all of life's important moments year after year.

We were inspired to open CEG bakery because of our first trip to Paris. The Parisian hospitality we experienced was reminiscent of the Southern hospitality we grew up on. The bakeries reminded us of being in our mother's kitchen: pastries made from scratch, intimate spaces, and most of all, personal connection. The ingredients were so simple but were put together with these complex flavor profiles. From the Belgian waffle stand with Nutella and Grand Marnier, to the buttered baguettes, you could just taste the love and admire the skill. The shop owners took the time to make us feel like a part of their community. We came as customers but left as family. Little did we know this trip was the catalyst for change that shook up our lives.

It would be a year before we stepped out on faith and went back to school for formal training at Le Cordon Bleu. Picture it, Labor Day 2010, poolside with our two-year-old niece sitting between us. We were discussing how lovely it would be to own a bakery or bed and breakfast and work there when we retire. We looked at each other and said, "Why wait for retirement?" Obviously, we did not! *CARPE DIEM*. We knew our degrees in fashion merchandising and biochemistry would not provide us with what we needed to expand beyond natural talent. It was important to obtain proper training in French techniques and learn important business insights for the food industry. We accomplished this while working full-time nine-to-five gigs. After work, we'd go to school from 6 pm to midnight, Monday to Friday. We did this for two years.

We left graduation ready to conquer the Atlanta baking scene; prepared with a great foundation and strong mentors. We had a plan. We had the skills. But even the most prepared person is still unprepared for the obstacles that small business owners face—and double that when you add the complexities of food service to the mix. In our case, there were the added layers of being a small, minority woman-owned business.

All these realities set in quicker than cement: lack of funding, lack of rest, death to our social life. We never discussed those things in school. Funding options (or shall we say a *lack* of funding options) made it so that we had to be self-funded for several years. The faith kicks in when you are faced with the choice to give up or keep going.

Because giving up is not in our DNA, we choose the latter. We slowly built our clientele by acquiring a Cottage Food license to produce out of our home. You know what that means: friends, family, and co-workers were our first customers. (Thanks to all those who allowed us to hone our skills on you!)

Then what happened? The orders we prayed for begin to come in, and we realized...*wow this is real*!

A home kitchen gets transformed quickly once you begin professionally baking. It is a whole different experience to bake professionally than it is for fun. Your space is sacrificed for housing 50-pound bags of sugar and flours, cake pans, cupcake pans, and sheet pans. All the utensils, gadgets, bowls, baking cups, and other essential baking items will fill your racks, and you must make sure everything is six inches off the ground.

Once you are officially a business, you realize you must wear so many hats, because there is no one else to put them on. After pairing that eye-opener with menu creation, pricing, and packaging, it got a bit overwhelming. We had so many needs, and so many questions. What does our brand look like? What do we want our packaging to say about us? Finding the right natural ingredients while balancing price and profit. Standing out. Finding our niche and unique customer base. How do we generate capital?

All these questions became and continue to be at the top of our minds. We learned this was part of the "entrepreneurial cycle:" 1. Focus 2. Concentration 3. Momentum 4. Stabilization. We would stay in the "focus" phase for several years.

Everything begins with action, and every action requires more faith. From opening our storefront in 2013, transporting to and from our rental kitchen space, to then building our own kitchen onsite after saving for eight years. *Faith.* From crying daily about bleeding money, to maneuvering and not only surviving but thriving through COVID. *Faith.* From the first 100-cupcake order to 1500 peach cobblers at a National Game. *Faith.*

When we say we "slay," we mean we are achieving something spectacular. How do we slay? We stay rooted in God. When you understand the source of everything that you have, and when you are grateful for everything, it creates a different mindset, a limitless mindset. We're not bound by limitations, fears, doubts, or even when the money looks funny. Nor are we distracted by haters. We always pray that everything we bake brings glory to God. That does not mean we will not have hard times or struggles (we have), but we know the Lord will have our back and get us through.

We stay true to ourselves and our vision for our business. Everybody has advice and if we listened to them all, we would be selling fried bologna sandwiches and other people's made-from-home specialties. We would be renting our space out for taxes and using shoe cake pans made from aluminum foil! When you have a vision, you can't allow other people's thoughts, opinions, or fears to change your vision. That doesn't mean we don't take advice; we just have to use discernment. We try not to compare ourselves to other businesses because every journey is different. We want to be successful; we just don't want to be anyone else. We want to stand the test of time, not just be on trend.

CEG is a place that makes everyone feel welcome. When you walk through our door, you're not just walking into a bakery: you're walking into an experience. You will feel the love as soon as you walk through the door; you will feel comfortable. Whether you have a good conversation, have a transformative food tasting, or meet a new connection, you will not leave this place feeling like just a customer. Simply put, it's the Parisian experience with Southern charm.

We believe in serving the community we service. We champion charities that support cancer, domestic violence, and children. We take treats to the domestic violence shelters and donate to various other charity events. We believe that supporting these charities, as well as supporting people like first responders, veterans, and our homeless community when they come hungry or thirsty into the shop, gives us a chance to give back and pay it forward. Service also includes giving advice to young or new entrepreneurs, and supporting other local small businesses to build a network of like-minded professionals.

We see ourselves having a cooking show as well as a show that showcases small women-owned businesses. A cookbook with new and reimagined recipes. More CEG locations, some cafés, and a restaurant down the line. A nonprofit organization mentoring new and young minority small business owners. Traveling the world trying new cuisines and bringing them back to Atlanta. Even a homeless hotel inspired by and named after our mother, Gladys, who always gave a helping hand to everyone she knew. We still don't know all that God has planned for us, but if you can achieve your dream without Him, your dream is too small!

Who is CEG Bakery? CEG is us, Glynnis and Katha. It is love through food. It is our customers that come through the door. It is the feeling you get when you have your first bite. It is our expression of God through baking. It is the warm and fuzzy environment. It is the sweet smell of fresh baked goods coming out the oven. It is God's presence that resides here. It is good conversation. It is the unknown yet to be discovered. It's more than a place. It is God's vision given to us.

Iced Tea, a Hug, and Divorce Papers

Imani Aieshah

Imani Aieshah is a Bronx girl living in Georgia, a creative spirit, a wife, mama, speaker, marriage coach, and author of *What Your Mama Didn't Tell You About Marriage.* She is passionately committed to helping married couples who feel they are on the brink of falling apart restore intimacy and friendship in their relationship. For seven years, she has worked with many couples all around the world and has seen firsthand how marriages can go from almost separated to connected and healthy.

The relationship clichés we've heard all our lives only limit a marriage. Imani guides you to creating a marriage that goes beyond those limits. Her signature coaching experiences give couples both the techniques and confidence to tackle the inevitable tough times and truly create the solid, long-lasting marriage they want. With her, you'll find the sweet spot that only your marriage has and feel comfortable enough to talk about anything, even the hard stuff, with less headache and more resolution and peace.

Imani is not only transparent about her own marriage journey, but she has created platforms, like her show, *The Sauce,* and her podcast, *The Saucy Marriage,* for other couples to share the truth in their journey as well. It is in her dedication to tearing down the shame around having marital issues that she has become a catalyst in the movement to change the negative narrative of "failure" around marriage to one of growth and freedom.

When she's not coaching, you can find her searching Instagram for plant-based recipes, running around with her kids, or watching shows with her hubby until he inevitably crashes at 8:31 pm.

Follow her on Instagram:
https://www.instagram.com/imaniaieshah/

———

It was like I just blacked out. As if I, nine months pregnant and ready to pop any day, was watching myself make moves from above with no way to control what was happening. My iced herbal tea went flying, and I couldn't even remember when I let it go. Our living room had become a movie scene. Hands and arms were flailing. The cacophony of shouting and confusion filled the air. Everything happened so fast, and yet it also seemed to be happening in slow motion. Honestly, it was all a blur. All I knew was that I had leaped from the couch, round and plump, to pull my parents away from each other before they could embrace. I didn't want them to hug, especially not then.

But, let's rewind the story just a bit.

It was November 2015, and I was pregnant with my first child. This was a big deal for my family; not just because it was the first grandchild for my parents, but also because this was all happening after a miscarriage the year before. I was a mixture of anxious stomach knots and utter excitement about becoming a mother. My own mother had come to support me on the journey, staying with us from my last month of pregnancy until my daughter, Sovereign, was four months old. However, the end of my pregnancy was met with news that shook up my life in a way I could have never expected.

It was then that my parents "divorced." And since I'm sure you're wondering why I've put that word in quotes, let's get into it. I am a child of twice-divorced parents. My parents actually divorced (*no quotations*) when I was 18. My mother had told me on a family weekend visit during my freshman year. I wasn't surprised or fazed by the decision then—in fact, I was glad they had finally decided to split up officially. They had been living like roommates for as long as I could remember. I had already cried all the tears I was going to cry. I had laid, stomach down, on that green carpet in our hallway listening to them throw words at each other like daggers more times than I could count. I was tired, too. And besides, I was off to college. Their distance would no longer take up space in my world.

For the next two years, I navigated the discomfort around parents who weren't talking to each other. But in that third year, something changed: My parents had somehow become friends. It happened slowly at first: a conversation here, a favor there. But it blossomed into a full-blown friendship. I had never seen my parents like this. They laughed together, hung out, talked, and as a family, we would all spend time together actually enjoying each other's company. By this time, I was out of college, and I was experiencing the kind of family dynamic I never had as a child. I was seeing my parents in a new light, and I fell in love with our little family. And as I began living my own young adult life, I found a love of my own.

I was a Bronx girl, back home from college in Atlanta, Ga. He was a Brooklyn boy who had returned home from a post-military life in Texas. We met, dated, spent two years long-distance while I went to graduate school back in Georgia, and eventually got engaged and married. When he asked my parents for my hand, he asked them both—together. He didn't have to go to each one separately because my parents had become an unconventional "we" again. They danced together at my wedding. They went grocery shopping together. They gave each other counsel. They helped and supported each other. And this man I was going to spend the rest of my life with got to experience my divorced parents in this beautiful way. It went on this way for eight years. Then, before I could even process what happened, it was over.

Just a week or so before the birth of my first child, my father suddenly announced to us that he was courting a woman and was in a relationship. Now, you may be thinking, *"So what? Your father was single and is entitled to his happiness. Why shouldn't he pursue a romantic relationship?"* And I agree. But it was much more complicated than that. It was a quick and surprising development that went from the announcement of courtship to a spontaneous wedding in a matter of weeks. Yes, he was free to make this decision for *his* life, but that did not mean it didn't have a profound effect on all of us going forward. Both can be true. And for me, there were emotional consequences to his announcement that came to a head that night in my living room.

My mother had been staying with us already in anticipation of the birth, and my dad came down the week I was supposed to have her. When he made his announcement a few days earlier, my parents stopped talking to each other, and when they did talk, it ended up in an argument. Determined to protect my peace before I went into labor, I had a discussion with both my parents about doing whatever they needed to do to be civil toward each other while they were both in Atlanta. They agreed. But that night, as we were all sitting on the couch, they got into an argument.

I don't remember how it started or what they said; I just remember it feeling heavy and sad. In an emotional moment amid the shouting, my mother asked my father to hug her. And something about that exchange, after everything, switched something in me. Without thinking, I lunged between them to prevent it. And I don't remember much after that except my father calling my husband from the back to carry my pregnant self out of the living room. Needless to say, my parents did not get into it again (at least not in front of me) the rest of the visit. Still, once I had my daughter and my father called a few days later to say that he just went and did it, went and got married, I knew I was about to go through another divorce. Except this time, I *was* hurt. This time, I *did* care. This time, it felt like I was in mourning.

At the time, I didn't know why the attempted hug triggered me so much. In hindsight, the request felt like a moment of desperation and pity. It all felt fake. For eight years, my parents had something that felt real to me, and in that instant, I felt it had been reduced to a figment of my imagination. It wasn't a hug born of healing or a tearful goodbye. It was not a heartfelt punctuation after finding a resolution through a tough transition. It was something else. A human moment. A need for touch and comfort that felt like it would not change anything. Looking back, whatever it was to me at that time, I regret robbing them of that moment with what was basically the outburst of my inner child. I wanted to simply blame it on the pregnancy hormones, but at 30 years old, I had to come to grips with the fact that this time I had to give myself time to mourn the loss of my parents' relationship. Like them, I had to heal.

Having this experience as an adult was a pivotal moment for me with regard to how I approach my own relationship of (now) 16 years, and the relationships of the couples I help as a marriage coach. The truth is, I had tried countless times to repair my parents' relationship as a child. I was a middle school peer conflict mediator, so in my young mind, if I could get a group of nine-year-olds to see each other's point of view at recess, I could help my parents too. But I couldn't. If their marriage was going to be repaired, it would have had to be because they were working to better understand themselves and each other with grace and honesty that didn't intentionally bite. Because that's essentially what marriage is—an opportunity to gain a heightened state of awareness of self, your spouse, and, as a result, your marriage as a whole. Because marriage ain't easy. I mean, it's a lifelong commitment to someone who will be changing, growing, and struggling through life while you're also changing, growing, and struggling through life. Shoot, that's enough to make your head hurt. It's a journey for sure, but that doesn't mean we can't enjoy the ride!

My husband and I don't just have a healthy, supportive marriage spontaneously. It is very intentional. We had to learn each other. Through miscarriages, job loss, bankruptcy, daggering words, and tears, we had to *choose* to *see* each other. And to this day, that allows us to see each other through some of the biggest challenges of our lives. Marriage is as real, as complicated, and as unique as the two people in it. And as a wife, mom, and coach, I never try to make it look like someone else's relationship.

The couples I work with don't deserve a cookie-cutter coach spouting clichés they could have just Googled, either. They deserve support and guidance that is unique to them. So, I coach them on how to design the marriage that works for them, how to communicate without the blame game, how to talk to each other without shutting down or going off even if they communicate completely differently, and how to fold fun and time together into their busy lives and crazy schedules. I know every couple won't stay together, but I also know many *can* with the right tools. *Til' death do us part* wasn't in the cards for my parents, but for the couples for whom it is (they just need some support in getting there), I've made it my mission to help them create a relationship legacy they are excited to show their children. I do it for them, for their children, and, if I'm being real, for the little girl in me with the twice-divorced parents.

A New Jersey Peach

Ashley Banks

Born and raised in Newark, NJ, Ashley Banks is the proud owner of a thriving salon where she specializes in hair extensions. She has a passion for transforming her vast clientele and boosting confidence. She has dedicated her career to mastering the art of extensions and helping new stylists get ahead early in their careers. Her commitment to excellence and success has taken her from New Jersey to Atlanta, Ga., and she is excited for the next chapter of her career.

Ashley is also a loving dog mom and crème brûlée connoisseur.

https://stan.store/AshleyBanksExtensions

———

My journey began in Newark, New Jersey, where I grew up with my family. It was a place filled with its own challenges, but it was also a space that shaped who I am today. My mother, a strong and determined woman, made a courageous decision that would change our lives—she moved us to Allentown, Pa. It was a bold step toward a brighter future, and I would come to realize how significant that choice was.

Moving to Allentown opened up new opportunities for my brother and me. My mother worked tirelessly to ensure we had what we needed, instilling in us the values of hard work and resilience. Those early years were foundational in shaping my character and aspirations. I focused on my education and graduated from high school. At the time I thought I'd move back to Jersey. But decided to enroll in college and pursue a psychology major.

However, as time went on, I found myself questioning whether college was the right fit for me. Despite my enthusiasm, I struggled to feel aligned with the academic pressures and responsibilities. After a year of soul-searching, I made the difficult decision to drop out. This choice drew mixed reactions from my family; some viewed it as a setback, while I saw it as the beginning of a journey to rediscover my true self.

After leaving college, my mom encouraged me to explore my interests and consider beauty school. Initially, I hesitated, holding onto the belief that there might not be much financial stability in pursuing a career in the beauty industry. However, my mother's belief in my potential pushed me to take a chance. I enrolled in beauty school, and what I discovered was a world filled with excitement and creativity. The ability to transform not only appearances but also the confidence of others was fulfilling. I thrived in this environment, learning new techniques and sharpening my skills. This experience wasn't just about technical knowledge; it was about rediscovering my passion and understanding the positive impact I could have on the lives of others.

I worked in a salon for about eight months before leaving. I wasn't making any money as a stylist. And I didn't have many bookings. I was discouraged. I started working at call centers and warehouses. I'd work a job and leave after about four to six weeks. I did this for years. Until one day on my break, I left work and never went back.

Years later I opened my own salon, Sew-In Love Extensions Bar, at the height of the pandemic. Launching a business during such uncertain times was risky, but I saw an opportunity to create a space where clients could find comfort and care. While many were retreating, I chose to step forward, and every challenge I encountered only fueled my determination to succeed. I poured my heart and soul into my salon, creating an environment where clients felt welcomed and empowered. As the years went by, my salon flourished, and with it, my confidence as an entrepreneur grew. Celebrating four years of success was not just about financial stability; it was a testament to my journey and the transformation I had undergone.

In September 2023, I made another bold decision—moving to Atlanta, Ga. This move was driven by my desire for greater freedom and the opportunity to expand my career. Atlanta, with its vibrant culture, black excellence, opportunities, and thriving beauty industry, presented an exciting landscape for my growth. I embraced this change wholeheartedly, looking forward to new possibilities, both personally and professionally. The move to Atlanta represented more than just a geographical shift; it was a shift in mindset. I was ready to explore new avenues, connect with diverse communities, and push the boundaries of my creativity. This new chapter is already enriching my life and career, reinforcing the belief that stepping out of one's comfort zone can lead to extraordinary experiences.

Throughout my journey, one lesson has profoundly resonated with me: the importance of believing in yourself and pursuing YOUR dreams. There were moments when self-doubt crept in, and the weight of challenges felt overwhelming. Yet, I learned that with hard work, dedication, and a belief in my abilities, I could overcome anything. My story serves as a reminder that dreams don't come true overnight; they require persistence, resilience, and the courage to chase what ignites your passion. The belief in my dreams has propelled me forward, even when the path seemed uncertain. I've come to understand that success is not merely about reaching a destination but about embracing the journey and the growth that comes with it.

As I reflect on my journey from Newark to Allentown and now to Atlanta, I am filled with gratitude for the experiences that have shaped me. My mother's support, the lessons learned through perseverance, and the belief in my dreams have all played vital roles in my transformation. As I continue this journey, I firmly believe that anyone can achieve their dreams if they are willing to work hard and dedicate themselves to their passions. My story is a testament to the power of resilience, the importance of self-belief, and the incredible potential that lies within each of us. If you dare to dream and put in the effort, anything is possible. The journey may be long and filled with challenges, but the rewards you get from believing in yourself and pursuing your passions are immeasurable.

My journey reflects the understanding that life is not just about the destination but about the experiences and growth we encounter along the way. Each step I took, each decision I made, and each challenge I faced contributed to the person I am today. I am proud of my roots and the journey that has brought me to this moment. I am excited about the future and the opportunities that lie ahead in Atlanta, where I can continue to grow, evolve, and inspire others to pursue their dreams. My story is proof that dreams, when paired with hard work and dedication, can indeed come true. As I navigate this new chapter of my life, I carry with me the lessons learned and the belief that anything is possible for those who believe in themselves.

A Love Like No Other

Cami Barnes

Cami Barnes is a wife, mom, ordained minister, wedding officiant, professional matchmaker, speaker, author, and leadership development coach.

She earned her bachelor's degree in psychology at Wright State University with a focus on industrial and organizational psychology, which is the study of employee behaviors in the workplace. She holds a master's of business administration degree from St. Thomas University, focused on human resources management. And she is currently a doctoral student, working toward a degree in theology and ministry.

Cami's career experience includes entrepreneurship, over a decade in human resources, as well as experience in the areas of mental health, social work and wellness, and has given her a unique framework from which she strategizes for teams and companies.

As CEO of Linked 4 Love Matchmaking, she is driven by her passion for fostering genuine connections among single, marriage minded professionals.

Her book, *Securing the B.A.G. (Big Audacious Goals)* is a tool that provides practical tips and a workbook for elevating to the next level of success. And her contribution to the *Deeper Women Teach: Volume 2* book provides the steps for leveraging your healing and self-care to reach your greatest potential.

With a heart for philanthropy and a testimony, she launched the Cami Barnes Scholarship Foundation Inc., which provides trauma survivors with funding to cover their college expenses.

Cami's education and experience has established a solid framework for her expertise. But it's her passion for empowerment that drives her life's work of motivating others to live out their dreams with courage and intention.

www.CamiBarnes.com
www.Linked4Love.co

———

I began my "Slaying Atlanta" journey as Cami Barnes, professional matchmaker, wedding officiant, motivational speaker, author, and coach. My meeting with Leigh Clark, our curator, was warm; we talked, shared stories, and laughed together. It felt more like a chat with an old friend than an interview to be a part of an anthology. Leigh and I share many commonalities, though it's likely that outside observers would see us as opposites. However, the power that comes from sharing our stories is that we connect with parts of our human-ness and it allows us to see that we are much more alike than we are different. Our stories can empower and inspire, they can validate and champion causes, the best thing about our stories is that they are a moving picture, continually changing as we grow and evolve.

During any moment or season of our lives, our stories are only as representative as the "where" and "who" we are in that moment. Leigh gave instructions and her description of what the *Slaying* series consists of—the stories of women entrepreneurs representing the cities they live and work in—and it resonated with me. Writing about that sounded easy enough. My primary business is called Linked 4 Love, and I provide professional matchmaking services that include personality assessments, image consulting, ongoing support through 1:1 calls, background checks, and career/relationship integration. I also provide wedding services. The wedding services my company provides include officiation, pre-marital relationship coaching, and photography/videography provided by my husband, Will Barnes.

When people ask me what brought me to matchmaking, I usually reply that I have a unique education and career background, as well as a specialized skillset I attained from those things, all of which make me well suited for it. Prior to starting my business as a professional matchmaker, I'd spent over a decade working in human resources. Before that, I held various roles in the mental health and social work fields. I have a bachelor's degree in psychology, certifications in professional matchmaking and relationship coaching, and by the time this story is published, I will have also attained a master of business administration degree in human resources management. I have been assessing people for strengths, weaknesses, mental health, personality traits, and goodness of fit, in one way or another, for my entire adult life. I am also a lover of love.

I have a natural inclination for helping people, and a trauma history that allows me to share a level of empathy with anyone seeking a safe, and healthy partner for romantic love. The trauma history is one of the ties that bind me with Leigh, during our initial meeting she shared with me that she was a domestic violence survivor. The totality of my career, education, and life experience drew me towards professional matchmaking. I wanted to assist people in finding love. Someone like me, and someone like Leigh, might have benefitted from the services of a professional matchmaker prior to finding ourselves in unhealthy, unsafe relationships. I am someone who can screen for things, assess potential matches on behalf of my clients, gather information, and support them through the process. These are all things that might have caught some of the red flags early on for me, Leigh, and the millions of other domestic violence victims in our individual experiences with toxic, abusive relationships.

It can be tough not to become jaded after being hurt, surviving trauma in situations where one was supposed to feel safe and loved. My heart has never hardened from any of the experiences I've had; my love of love has kept me open and decidedly optimistic that real love exists, in a healthy way that I and everyone else deserve. That mindset, along with an extensive healing journey is what allows me to stand, presently, as a wife who's happily been with my husband for over nine years. Having my business, Linked 4 Love, has revealed that so many people are looking for love and desire a marriage that seems just out of their reach. There are many reasons for this; some people believe they are ready to be in a relationship, to be a good partner to someone, but they simply do not have the skillset for it. (I decided to use "skillset" here as a funny nod to my human resources background, but it's accurate.)

Matchmaking and workforce recruitment are almost mirror images. In one role, I would be assessing candidates' goodness of fit for a career or position with a company; the other role requires me to assess potential matches and their goodness of fit for my client demographic, "marriage-minded professionals." In a work setting, skills and duties are required for every job that a company has available. In a relationship, skills and duties are also required to be a good partner to any potential match, especially if the ultimate goal is marriage. This is where coaching can be helpful.

The 2024 dating landscape is different. Most of my clients fall into two groups; one group of clients are successful in their careers but put so much time into their success that they haven't prioritized finding a mate. The other group consists of people who were previously married, divorced, or widowed and have found themselves back on the dating scene with no idea how to date. The biggest challenge for me as a matchmaker has been that I can do everything possible on my end to ensure a good match, but when you are in the business of "people," it's not possible to account for every possible scenario. Just when I think I've covered all the bases, a situation arises and I'm like, "Wow...OK, this is new," and I have to add or adjust my policies accordingly. Life is a journey; business is a journey. You must stay flexible and agile and adapt quickly to be able to navigate the changes, pros, cons, ebbs, and flows that come along with life and entrepreneurship.

I am in the business of love. But this has nothing to do with why I chose the title "A Love Like No Other" for my chapter. I mentioned early on that our stories change, grow, and evolve as we do. For me, "A Love Like No Other" has shifted me in a new and unexpected direction. I am not the same "me" I was when I started out as a part of this project. And after thinking long and hard about how I wanted to frame those changes, I decided that sharing this new thing was just as relevant to my chapter because I would feel like a counterfeit sharing my story in a way that doesn't capture where I am now.

The biggest part of my shift began when I was ordained to officiate weddings. To do that, I had to be ordained as a minister. And though, in the beginning, my thought process regarding that step was specifically to officiate weddings, and as a compliment to my matchmaking business, something unexpected happened. I had always considered myself a woman of faith, a Christian. I've been active in various forms of ministry most of my life, from growing up in a Baptist church and singing in the children's/youth choir, Sunday school, vacation Bible school in the summers, to being an adult who is active in outreach, evangelism, and prayer ministries. I ran a nonprofit organization for five years that I considered to be a ministry, which provided supportive services to domestic violence survivors. I've been a motivational speaker for three years, and I've always felt the most in my element when I was able to share elements of my faith with the audiences. But I never wanted to be a minister in the format of preacher or pastor.

Though there were people who spoke lovingly to me, telling me that they saw that in my future, the title of "minister" always felt too big and heavy for me, so I had zero desire for it. And when I became ordained, I ran from the title, even though that's what my certificate said. I announced on my social media profiles that I'd been ordained as a "wedding officiant." I didn't want the judgment and preconceived notions that people would lump on me if I used the title of "minister." But something happened that changed that perspective. I felt God calling me higher, and that title of "minister" combined with my love of God opened my heart to submit completely to where He was directing me. And now, in addition to the titles I shared in the first line of the text, I have openly and unashamedly accepted the title of "minister." In so many ways, God has been using me as an instrument of His love, and it is His transformative love that leads me...now more than ever before.

Nothing is Normal Anymore

Paula Campbell

With over two decades of experience, Paula Campbell has driven over $3 billion in revenue across industries such as fintech, e-commerce and AI. A seasoned revenue leader, she has recently launched Swag Boss, an up-and-coming retail motivation brand, fulfilling her passion for inspiring others. Paula is also a proud mother of two adult children and excitedly awaiting her first grandchild. An animal lover and great friend, Paula is deeply committed to mentoring and uplifting others. In addition, she works as a business strategist and consultant, helping brands of all sizes achieve success.

Instagram: @PaulaCampbell, @theofficialswagboss
Facebook: https://m.facebook.com/paulaanncampbell/
TikTok: @therealswagboss
LinkedIn: https://www.linkedin.com/in/paulacampbell

———

2020 was a challenging year for everyone, and for my family and me, it brought unprecedented difficulties. We were navigating the early days of the pandemic when disaster struck—our house caught fire. That day marked the beginning of the end of life as I knew it.

Having already endured a decade of childhood sexual abuse, poverty, and homelessness while pregnant in the '90s, I had worked hard to rebuild my life. I climbed from telemarketing to a successful career in sales, ultimately becoming a CRO. My life seemed stable: I had a loving partner, a graduated daughter, my son turning 18, and a warm, bustling household. But everything changed on September 14th with the fire.

As we faced displacement amid the pandemic's chaos and supply chain issues, we thought things couldn't get worse. However, on September 28th, a doctor's visit revealed that my husband Todd had a 4x6-inch mass in his chest. The diagnosis was cancer, though its origins and progression were unknown.

On October 22nd, Todd underwent emergency surgery due to fluid in his chest. The surgeons warned us that survival was uncertain. Thankfully, he made it through, but our struggles were far from over. We grappled with displacement, insurance, contractors, and the constant stress of Todd's illness.

By Christmas, Todd had passed away, making it the worst day of my life. Just eight months later, my mother, who had struggled with severe bipolar disorder and a tumultuous relationship with me, also died. Despite her harshness, I mourned her loss deeply.

The following is a post I shared only three months before Todd passed, illustrating what it was like and how I was feeling at that time...

———

I'm sharing a few insights and baring my soul about my experience being a partner in my husband's cancer journey... well, let's not be that nice... cancer hell! I hope this will help other partners in the fight.

Cancer is referred to as a "battle" because it truly feels like a fight. It's hard to understand that in its truest form when you haven't been in the battle this closely... but once you're in it, it makes sense. I think of cancer as this beast who disappears briefly and just when you think he's gone... turns out he was just reloading. *Clack! Clack!*

Again, I'm speaking from my experience here. I can't speak on Todd's experience. His is much different and unique from mine even though we are going through it together. He is living with this beast in his body. He is in chemo, he is tired, he is vomiting, he is sick. His perspective is by default going to be deeper and more personal than mine.

We had an electrical fire in our house on September 14, 2020, and two weeks later we were introduced to a 4x6-inch mass in Todd's chest. We were displaced from September 14th to April 1st, and between hotels and an apartment. COVID had slowed down supply chains, so everything took longer than usual. So, in addition to my number one priorities which were now Todd and cancer, I was contending with living arrangements, four dogs, my mom, my son, contractors, insurance, and disaster cleanup, all while getting ready for chemo and learning about the rarity of his cancer in the midst of a pandemic. Then one of our dogs passed in January, and I lost my job in February. It was a very overwhelming time.

This experience has changed my life forever. I'm literally just going to spout some thoughts in bullets that I think of at times or have worried about. Maybe my experience will help someone else feel more normal about their own—when absolutely NOTHING IS NORMAL ANYMORE.

1. Nothing is normal anymore. Life has truly been flipped upside down. Everything we knew to be our regular life was suddenly overtaken by illness. Serious illness. It hasn't been the same since. My home, my marriage, my career—all rock solid, all of which I worked hard to make stable, and suddenly those three most stable components of my life were in peril.

2. Todd was gone mentally for quite a while, and I didn't expect that. I never knew cancer would make me grieve so many times. After years of being joined at the hip, suddenly he was with me, but he wasn't with me. Chemo has so many side effects, and cognitive impairment is one of them. I love my husband's soul—it's why I fell in love with him—but I couldn't see him behind his eyes anymore. My heart broke every time I tried to tell him something and he couldn't understand me. I slept on the couch at the apartment the entire time we were there because he really needed to lay whatever way was best for him. Our nights of going to bed together for years suddenly stopped, and I lost my husband's companionship completely for at least five months. My heart hurt.

3. Sleep deprivation allows your mind to go anywhere and everywhere, and it's out of your control. People who love you try to offer advice: go to sleep, take melatonin, get on a pill, whatever. And while all of that is valid, it doesn't change the fact that you're afraid to go to sleep. The thoughts of what is happening now, fears about what is going to happen, and the grief around the losses you've already experienced and are currently experiencing make sleep very difficult. The sheer level of violence and consistency behind the vomiting made me terrified for Todd. I was afraid to sleep sometimes because I wanted to make sure he was OK all night— sneaking in and out of the room so I didn't disturb him but making sure he was still OK. It reminded me of when my

kids were newborns, and I could hear every gurgle they made from rooms away. I lost a full two nights of sleep MINIMUM a week between October and, well... now.

4. The Responsibilities you normally share are all added to your plate. Example: I take care of our finances and household stuff and Todd used to take care of our cars and the dogs. It occurred to me that I should have checked the tag renewal dates while I was getting pulled over for an expired tag last month. It was especially challenging during all of the moving back and forth but I kept it from him as much as I could. He felt so bad he couldn't help, so I would get him settled in first and then go do the stuff that needed to be done. This one is not a big deal—it's just a stark change to how I had to adjust managing time and responsibilities because there was so much to do at that time with chemo, countless ER visits, work, and all the drama associated with the house fire. They weren't the types of things anyone else could help with (contractors, insurance, floor tiles, disaster cleanup, etc.)

5. The pandemic makes this suck more! I couldn't have drinks with a friend, get my hair done, or take a break from cancer outside of driving my car. I stayed fully isolated because I could NOT expose his weakened immune system to anything! It was a very lonely time before vaccines happened.

6. Then there were the things I have and do wonder along the way:

a. Will we ever get our life back... together?

b. When will he understand what I'm saying again?

c. Will the neuropathy go away?

d. What do you mean the cancer relapsed in six weeks? He hasn't even recovered from chemo yet! (There's that *clack clack* I spoke of earlier.)

e. What can I cook today that he can taste?

f. How can I help him gain weight?

g. All the ways I keep these tears inside my face when I'm with him, so he doesn't see my sadness.

h. Are we ever going to be able to put cancer behind us?

i. He slept through most of the football games last season... when will we swing towels together again?

j. Will we sleep together again?

k. Why are we going through this?

l. Are we EVER GOING TO GET OUR LIFE BACK???

———

Coping with how to win from here on while loss was the headliner was my goal. Self-care and attitude have been key.

I've spent almost three years moving from place to place trying to find my place in the world where it's just me. Building my brand, Swag-Boss, has been forefront while I work to finance my efforts.

You can stay up while life is down. It's all in the attitude, reaction, and response to what life presents. What I've learned is that life is unpredictable. You can do everything right and overcome all obstacles, and life will do things that you cannot control. We have to control our minds. It's the power we have.

Swag-Boss is about overcoming odds and maintaining your personal swag. No excuses. You got this!

Reflections Beyond the Chair

Hannah Evans

My name is Hannah Evans, and I was raised in Washington, D.C. Growing up in a city with a big family (six sisters, three brothers) exposed me to a plethora of different fashion trends, art, music, and hairstyles. I've been married since 2005, and I have two daughters. In 2017, my family and I relocated to Georgia. I brought my city trends and flare to the south side of Atlanta, GA, and opened my own Salon Suite in 2019.

I started my career in the hair industry in 2001 and immediately fell in love with hair color and extensions. I strive to stay up-to-date with current trends and the newest techniques through continuous education. In 2012, I was the Northeast color educator for a hair brand. In addition, I am certified in multiple hand-tied extension methods, including Invisible Beaded Extensions, Laced Hand-Tied Extensions, and Hand-Tied Manes. These methods create the healthiest and optimal results for clients.

www.hairchaosstudio.com
https://www.instagram.com/hairchaos_studio/
https://www.tiktok.com/@itschaotic_hair
https://www.facebook.com/myhairchaos

———

The road to get me to Atlanta, Ga., hasn't been easy. I have always lived wild and free, beating my own drum, as they say. Art has always been a passion of mine. Growing up, my artistic eye led me to love photography. I learn better when working with my hands. In my early twenties, my artistic journey pivoted into a passion for hair. I soon realized color was it for me. Everything about transforming someone with color just excited me.

While trying to navigate my way through my hair career, who would've thought I would meet my husband on a blind date? I spent four years as an army wife, and while he was gone on deployment for 15 months, I worked at a local salon. When he returned home in 2007, I had a newborn baby in tow, and shortly thereafter we moved back to Washington, D.C. We were

40

both trying to figure out what was next for our careers. I worked in salons; then I became the Northeast color educator for a hair brand. Teaching other stylists, connecting, and networking became something that slowly grew into other loves.

After a few years of constant traveling, I decided it was time to get back behind the chair. I missed connecting with clients. Soon after, in January of 2015, my father passed away suddenly. This devastating loss took a toll on my family. I had never experienced such a great loss. Navigating through the feelings of grief, and trying to heal from that was difficult. In the middle of 2017, we relocated to the south side of Atlanta. This relocation forced me to start over, start fresh. So I adjusted my service offerings and figured out how to excel at those services. After years working in a commission-based salon, I felt it was time to take a leap of faith and open my own. In 2019, I finally opened my salon.

They say if you love what you do you will never work again, but I think that's a lie: You work harder. Who knew photography would come back into my life to help grow my business in the hair world? Blending these two passions has helped me share different parts of my salon and client experience, as well as my day-to-day work life. But most of all, it has allowed me to express who I am. I want to establish connections with my clients, and this goes beyond just giving a service. They become significant friendly faces we see regularly, and we have great talks that go beyond hair. We learn about them, their families, and work lives. As a stylist, I see some of my guests more than they see their doctors and therapists, and we see them throughout different phases and stages of their lives. We have watched them grow up through high school, marriage, babies, and so on. In addition, the hair industry is one of the only industries where we are allowed to touch them and be in their personal space.

Purpose, Passion, & Platform

Brittney Q. Hill

Brittney Q. Hill, originally hailing from Los Angeles, Calif., has been in the business of entertainment for almost 20 years, as an actress, entertainment executive, podcast host, and speaker.

Upon graduating and receiving her B.A. in mass media communications and film from The University of North Carolina at Charlotte, Brittney decided to pursue a career in entertainment full-time. Since then, she's worked alongside stars like Denzel Washington, Magic Johnson, Lynn Whitfield, and many others. To date, Brittney has graced many stages and screens, having accumulated over 25 credits on IMDb, but most notably recognized as *Lifetime's* Leading Lady, starring in several movies on the network.

In addition to acting, Brittney is the founder and CEO of Faith and Fame®, an entertainment media brand and podcast that bridges the gap between faith and entertainment.

Website: www.faithandfame.com
Instagram: https://www.instagram.com/brittneyqhill/?hl=en
Instagram for Faith and Fame:
https://www.instagram.com/faithandfametv/
Facebook: https://www.facebook.com/BrittneyQuianna/
Facebook for Faith and Fame:
https://www.facebook.com/FAITHandFAMETV
YouTube: https://www.youtube.com/@BrittneyQHill

———

Originally hailing from the city of Los Angeles, and now slaying the streets of Atlanta, I'm Brittney Q. Hill, a woman of many talents, but primarily an actress, entertainment executive, and entrepreneur. You may have seen me star in a few *Lifetime* movies, or as the face of my media brand and podcast, Faith and Fame®. A lot of my life's work is heavily focused on bridging the gap between faith and entertainment. I've been in the business of entertainment for almost 20 years. And what I've found over the last two decades is that there is a great disparity between the worlds of entertainment and faith. From my experience over the years, when you work on the ministry side of faith, you cross a lot of people who think Hollywood is "the devil's playground." And then on the opposite side of the spectrum, in the world of entertainment, you have people who'll tell you, "Don't talk about faith and God over here." At least that's how it was before Faith and Fame was born. And now it has become my life's mission and purpose to not only bridge the gap between faith and entertainment, but to show you how it's done.

I was a busybody growing up. There was no such thing as rest in the Hill household, because I kept my parents busy! I was a hip-hop dancer and even did a little ballet, jazz, and tap. I was also an athlete for fifteen years. I played basketball, ran track, and had my stint with soccer, softball, and volleyball. When one sport's season ended, I jumped right into the next one. I can't forget to mention pageantry. I was a beauty queen, and competed in pageants for over a decade, winning several regional titles and competing at the state level in the Miss Universe Organization. If I wasn't on a court or a field, I was on a stage. I was bound to be in the spotlight; born a natural performer.

But there was one particular performance that changed the entire trajectory of my life. I remember it like it was yesterday. I was in the fourth grade, and I was preparing to perform in my school's talent show for the first time. Usher had just dropped his hit single, "You Make Me Wanna," and one of my closest friends and I had partnered up to do a dance together. We spent weeks rehearsing, and had the choreography from the music video down PAT. On the day of the show, there were two shows scheduled. The first show in the morning was for students and staff, and the second show that evening was for family and friends.

But of course, life likes to throw curveballs when we least expect it. And on the day of the show, my friend bailed on me, she got scared. But what do you do in this situation? Do you just quit too, and throw away all your hard work? So I had to make a decision. Was I going to allow someone else's fear to stop me from doing what I was prepared to do? And at the tender age of nine, I had to learn quickly, THIS is what separates the good from the GREAT. So I did it. I got on that stage...and I FROZE. All that hard work and preparation, down the drain. Because if you're not careful of the company you keep, the thoughts, opinions, and fears of other people can paralyze you too. I had rehearsed this dance for days and weeks. I KNEW I was ready for that stage. But because of my friend's fear and reservations, I started to question myself.

Well after that painful first show, I went home and told my family about what happened. And just like the people who love you are supposed to do, they lifted me back up. They encouraged and affirmed me. And this is why who you have around you when you fail matters. Are you surrounded by people who like to kick you when you're down, or are they picking you back up?

Now don't forget, I still had a second performance, and my whole family was going to be there. So we arrived at the auditorium that night, and everybody was moving so fast to get good seats inside. As if things couldn't get any worse than that morning, when my sister was getting out of the car, she didn't realize I was right behind her and slammed my finger in the car door. That may have truly been the most excruciating pain I've ever felt in my life. We didn't know if my finger was broken, or even still intact. But once I got free, I distinctly remember my mom looking me square in the eye and asking me, "Do you still want to do this?" What a powerful question. And at that moment, I realized something that I would have to remember for the rest of my life. When you are walking in your purpose, opposition is going to come. When you make a declaration, and give God your *yes*, you better be ready for the opposition that's coming next. You might lose friends. People may slander you, ridicule you, envy, and hate on you. You might experience pain. You become a target. But that shouldn't discourage you, it should encourage you. Because that is your indication, that you are exactly on the path you're supposed to be. So I looked at my Mom, with the confidence of a girl who knew God was on her side, and said, "Yes, I want to do this." And I've been killing it ever since.

But being a woman of many talents, I've often been told that I need to decide who I'm going to be, that I could NOT be all of the above. Pick one, they said. And I really struggled with this idea of having to choose one thing over the other, because if I wasn't called to do ALL the things that God has graced me to do, then why would He give me all these gifts to begin with? Why would He present these platforms and opportunities? Now every opportunity is not a good opportunity, and that's where we need to exercise discernment. But when you KNOW it's God, why would you forfeit anything He's already endorsed?

What has helped me in my walk with destiny, was defining the difference between my PURPOSE, my PASSION, and my PLATFORM. They are not all the same, but they all work in tandem together. Let me share.

PURPOSE. Your purpose is not the thing that you DO. It is not your hobby, or your craft. Your purpose is about what happens to others when you do the thing you've been called to do. Your purpose is your mission statement. It is the overall umbrella of WHY we do the things we do. And your purpose will never be about YOU. Your purpose will always be in service to God, and the people who have been assigned to you. It is your GIFT to the world.

PLATFORM. Your platform is wherever God uses you to deliver your message and your ministry. Your ministry is also the thing you've been called to do. It's what we consider our craft. Your platform may change depending on the season, but your purpose, the umbrella, will remain the same. Your platform could be a classroom, a stage, maybe even your own house. Maybe you're a stay-at-home mom. Even that is a ministry. Your platform is the space and place used to fulfill your PURPOSE. But make no mistake about it, whatever platform God calls you to, in whatever season you find yourself in, it belongs to Him. He's just trusting you with it.

And the final "P" is for <u>PASSION</u>. Passion is the God-given desire that compels us to make a difference in a particular area of life or ministry. And I can assure you, when you're walking in purpose, not only will you have the passion to pursue it, but it will also fill your cup, even if it gets uncomfortable at times. That's how good God is. That even in the midst of challenge, stretching, and pruning, He will still fill your cup.

I want to leave you with this. It's my favorite quote by Erma Bombeck. It says, "At the end of this life when I stand before God, I would hope that I would not have a single bit of talent left, and I could say I used everything you gave me." I would further this sentiment by adding, I used my purpose, passion, and platform to serve You, and the people you assigned to me. And in return, I would hope He would look back at me and say, "Well done, my good and FAITHFUL servant." Matthew 25:2

3 Guiding Principles for a Meaningful Life:

Grit, Gratitude, and Grace

Loreal LeGate

Even as a child, Loreal LeGate was driven, understanding from a young age that to make her dreams happen she had to make her own way. Money was tight—she and her brother were raised by a single mother—so she focused on academics, earning an undergraduate degree in multinational business operations and, two decades later, a master's in international business.

The focus on global business was deliberate, fueled by a desire to travel and a fascination with different countries and cultures. After spending most of her career at a Fortune 100 financial services company (and traveling all over the world), she founded i3MKTG, a consulting practice that provided marketing strategy and communications for global nonprofits and trade associations.

Throughout her corporate and consulting career, Loreal has also progressed her personal passion: raising awareness and funds for nonprofit organizations with a mission to support women's economic empowerment in underdeveloped countries. The goal is to break the cycle of poverty by enabling opportunities for ongoing income through employment, agribusinesses, or microbusinesses.

Her passion, mixed with business acumen, has been used on advisory councils and a board of directors. She has traveled internationally to visit field projects. And, her last academic endeavor was to earn a certificate in nonprofit management from Harvard's Extension School.

Fun Facts:

- Loreal has visited 65 countries and all seven continents
- Family, friends, and colleagues have nicknamed her "Wonder Woman" and continually add to her Wonder Woman collection
- She donated a kidney to her brother, who is now doing great

LinkedIn: www.linkedin.com/in/loreal
Web: www.risinglotusfoundation.org

———

Grit, Gratitude, and Grace

These three words encapsulate a philosophy of life that balances accomplishment, appreciation for what one has, and the compassion to help others. Together they form my personal mantra and reflect how I aim to live my life.

Grit

Grit is the courage to follow your passion. It is determining goals and rising above challenges until you accomplish the desired outcome.

I have always been curious about the world. As a child, I would pretend to travel to other countries with my stuffed animals. I wanted to meet interesting people and learn about their cultures. Little did I know how much this passion would influence my life, my career, and my humanitarian endeavors.

My brother and I were raised by a single mom, and we did not have the means to travel. At school, the closest I could get to anything remotely international was to take Spanish classes. So, when it was time for university, I was thrilled to find a degree that focused on international business. Multinational business operations was my major, with a focus in marketing. I did not have a clear idea of what my ideal job would be, or which company I would work for, or even the industry. I just wanted a position where I could help companies grow their businesses internationally, and opportunities to travel the world.

The first two companies I worked for out of university were international, Fortune 500 companies. I held positions in business development, marketing, and communications. I excelled, won awards, and expanded my skills but was disappointed that neither provided the opportunity to travel outside the United States.

During this time, I married my college sweetheart, paid off his school debt, built a house, and had a child. We were always on the move for my husband's job, living in three states and six homes. Then at 30, I found myself as a single mom raising my beautiful six-year-old daughter. I was heartbroken, but determined that, no matter what life threw at us, we would not only survive but thrive. Lauren was a blessing and my greatest joy.

We moved from North Carolina back to Atlanta, Ga., and bought a small house in the best school district I could find. Leveraging my network, I landed an amazing position at a Fortune 100 financial services company where I spent almost 20 years. Through the years, I held positions in different business units to increase my knowledge and perspective in the financial services industry. Collaborating with savvy business and technology professionals was challenging and helped build my skills. Professional development courses helped refine them.

And finally, I was able to travel the world for client meetings, conferences, and trade association events.

I worked hard and did well, proud that my accomplishments were recognized through awards and promotions. But I was not done building a foundation for the next phase of my career. In my forties, I accomplished a long-time goal of completing a master's of international business at Georgia State University. It took five years of night classes balanced with work demands and raising my daughter, but I did it with determination.

Gratitude

Gratitude is recognizing the good in life, appreciating the contributions of others, and celebrating the triumphs. Gratitude leads to contentment and fulfillment.

I am not saying my work life was easy. I often worked long hours, needed bigger budgets, more staff, and less office politics. However, I have so much to be grateful for, starting with career opportunities that allowed me to take care of my children (my daughter and three stepdaughters from my second marriage).

I'm grateful to world leaders who live(d) their lives with purpose; they inspire me. Mother Teresa gave up life's comforts to serve those most in need. Her work spanned 130 countries and had a major impact. Melinda French Gates turned her wealth and influence into a progressive philanthropic movement.

Still, it's everyday women who really inspire me. These are women who are not looking for fame, who overcome all sorts of roadblocks to raise a family, support their communities, and make a difference. These unsung heroines may fly under the radar, but they are the bedrock of every society.

I'm grateful to my global clients and colleagues around the world who inspired me. Collaborating on strategy, growing business, and celebrating successes with them was fulfilling.

I'm grateful to family and friends who encouraged and supported me through the years. Especially my parents who built my confidence by telling me, "You can be anything you want to be when you grow up," and encouraged me to further my education.

Most of all, I'm grateful to my mom for all the sacrifices she made while raising my brother and me. No matter how much we struggled financially, she always managed to find a way to help others in need. It instilled in me a deep sense of compassion and a responsibility to help others.

As a teenager, I decided that helping women and their families would be a priority when I grew up. This has been the primary focus of my philanthropic efforts throughout my corporate and consulting career.

Grace

Grace is giving kindness to others and ourselves. It's the spirit of compassion for others and the generosity of goodwill.

Winston Churchill said, *"We make a living from what we do, we make a life from what we give."* My personal mission has been to champion women's economic empowerment. The need is staggering. Two billion people around the world live in poverty, living on less than $3.20 per day. Most lack the necessities that we take for granted: food and water security, housing, and medical care. Economic empowerment involves breaking the cycle of poverty by increasing access to income-generating resources and opportunities, including skills training, financial services such as microloans, and technology.

The goal of economic empowerment is to enable these women to achieve ongoing earned income through employment, small agribusinesses, or microbusinesses. When women contribute to their family's income, it fosters a cycle of prosperity that ripples out to benefit entire communities—and it has a lasting, intergenerational impact.

To support my mission, I have served on advisory councils and chaired a board of directors. I traveled internationally to visit projects and provided pro bono marketing strategy services.

To hone my skills in the nonprofit area, I earned a certificate in nonprofit organizational management from Georgia Center of Nonprofits and more recently a certification in nonprofit management from Harvard Extension School.

In 2015, I transitioned full-time to the nonprofit industry. I started i3MKTG, a consulting practice that provided marketing strategy and communications for global nonprofit organizations and trade associations.

These days, my focus is solely on raising awareness and funds for women's economic empowerment. My mom, daughter, and I co-founded the Rising Lotus Foundation (risinglotusfoundation.org). Our mission is to help women from low socioeconomic backgrounds, not just survive, but thrive. We partner with global nonprofit organizations to provide training, technology, resources, and opportunities to women so they can support themselves and their families.

Imparting Insights

I encourage you to follow your passion by focusing on the things that matter most in your life. With grit, gratitude, and grace, you too can achieve your goals. Below are a few tips that may help as you move forward:

- **Focus** – Where focus goes, energy flows. Few careers follow a straight path. And life is a crazy, curvy road. Keep your focus and energy directed toward your highest priorities so you can achieve them.
- **Plan** – Making a roadmap with goals, actions, and timelines is a good start. This will help you articulate your mission and organize actions.
- **Use your Superpower** – Identify the talent, skills, or qualities that make you unique. These are your superpowers. Leverage them to tell your story and achieve your goals.

- **Communicate** – The more you share your mission with others, the more ideas, resources, and opportunities will present themselves.
- **Collaborate** – Build a network by identifying and collaborating with people who share your passion. "Alone we can do so little, together we can do so much," Helen Keller said.
- **Grow** – Commit to lifelong learning. Continually building knowledge and skills is essential in both your work life and personal life.
- **Seek inspiration** – Think about who inspires you, and why. It could be someone famous or an everyday person who you admire. Model their behavior.
- **Mentor** – Find a mentor or business coach for guidance. And, once you have accomplished your dream, turn around and mentor others.

.

The Call to Atlanta: A City of Unseen Growth

Kayla Lemon

Kayla Lemon is a licensed realtor serving both the Atlanta Metropolitan and Middle Georgia area. Holding a bachelor's degree in healthcare administration, Kayla worked for a corporate healthcare company at a hospital for more than two years before deciding to make a career change that was more fulfilling to her, that she was passionate about. She wanted something more in alignment that caused her to dream bigger than what she was exposed to growing up. Now she strives to close the generational wealth gap by educating and helping people become first-time homeowners and real estate investors. When she is not busy in the field of real estate, she enjoys spending time with loved ones and practicing self-care.

IG: dathingirl
LinkedIn: Kayla Lemon Realtor

———

"Hey, this is ___ from ___ calling to let you know your lease application has been approved."

I got off the phone blinking. Not excited nor relieved. More so in a state of *I don't know how but I know God will.*

I got this phone call after ending a fast where I'd been seeking God's direction for where He wanted me to go next. When I first applied, I said to myself, "If this is where God wants me to go next, I know He will provide."

Getting this green light made up for every dark day I'd been through two years before when I was fighting the flow of the direction of my life. My instant thoughts were: *Was little 'ole me really going to be starting all over again and moving to Atlanta?* This was a city where I never wanted to live, yet I also knew it had so many opportunities for growth. Atlanta had been tugging on my heart for over a year after a depressing temporary move to Atlanta, but I knew this next move would require more from me. I would need to finally get out of my own way to grow into a person who could not only take on Atlanta, but also become the person God was calling me to be.

In 2022, I had quit my job and moved to Atlanta temporarily. Everything I tried doing my way or holding onto fell apart because I was still holding onto an older version of myself.

Prior to moving this second time in 2024, I learned so much about myself that I probably would not have learned if I had just surrendered to God's plan the first time. But I also looked at how the lessons prepared me to become a fuller version of myself and drew me closer to God.

My journey to Atlanta was not easy—and I don't want people to think it was. Instead, I hope they can see my journey as the presence of God moving in my life as a result of obedience. I was disobedient at one time, in that I did not want to accept what God was doing. I was disobedient in not wanting to leave things behind—things that I thought made me *me*. But all along, I knew I wanted a better quality of life. The environments I was once praised in would not be the environments where the "new" me could emerge. This I knew, but I did not know how (or if) I could stay true to an outdated version of myself that made me face a dark depressing internal battle that took me on a journey of questioning who I was.

Who am I? I knew that the answer to this question did not involve success, titles, or physical appearance, but there would be a *moment* that defined who I am. I had achieved a level of success that many would be proud to have, but deep down I was empty, and I understood that money really doesn't buy happiness. It does, however, provide stability in the environments that help you heal.

Financial stability has always been my driving force. I was raised by a single mother of five in public housing, and we lived paycheck to paycheck. College was my only opportunity for a better life; all I knew was that I was supposed to go to college and get a good job. I did that. I now have two degrees and was blessed with an entry-level position before I turned 25. After years of hard work, I finally felt like I'd made it, but quickly learned that degrees don't teach you how to heal from the moments that define you.

My whole outer identity was this hood and country skinny girl. I considered myself a poster child for making it out the legal way. Where I'm from—or from what I've seen—most make it out through hustling, which is slang for selling drugs or taking a man's money. But here's the thing... I became pregnant at 19, left my hometown, and started my own little mini-family. I had my own identity outside of motherhood and my relationship, but I kept who I truly was hidden from the world, and only shared myself with small groups of people who I trusted. Betrayal by old friends subsequently showed me the *me* I was hiding was the little girl who needed healing, but would also transform me into the woman who would get on the path God had aligned for me.

My inner self was always that little girl who knew she could have a better life than the one she came from, but did not want people to know her "why." That's why I always worked so hard—

not because I had to. All my man wanted me to do was look after our daughter and clean up, but the little girl in me always knew that when I left I would not move back, and that eventually I'd want my family to come with me.

That's why I began learning how to invest in real estate. My plans were to purchase a property, and then later use the income to purchase my mom a home. Indeed, God's plans were greater than mine. I asked him for growth to become better. He started placing opportunities in my path that would cause me to dream bigger.

But what is that new level for someone who never had a dream? I had to come to terms with the fact that I was still a little girl in an adult body. So my question was: how do I heal but also become who God called me to be? I had to focus on one thing, and God started handling the others. My one thing was becoming.

The difference between 2015 and 2022 was this: In 2015, I became a mom and *had* to change, but in 2022 I was seeking change and *wanted* to grow as a woman. In 2022, God made me uncomfortable in all areas of my life. He tested my faith, relationships, and responses. It was the uncomfortableness and uncertainty that caused me to move to Atlanta the first time. I felt I needed a break to just breathe and focus.

I still look back on that first break and ask God for forgiveness, because I felt as if I did it wrong. I knew God was making me uncomfortable on purpose by pushing me to move, but I did not want to let go of everything I felt made me in the process. Each step I took harboring resentment for those who could not just understand eventually brought me to a wall of truths. I can't say that this was shame, because I own every struggle whether financial or mental. But a wall of truths is better than this. Whatever I was going through when I finally came face to face with that wall was a result of my not letting go beforehand. When I hit rock bottom, that wall instantly became a mirror. I knew there was only one way to go, and that was whatever path God led me on.

What I didn't know was that God would use entrepreneurship to nudge me. My entrepreneurial journey quickly became a personal, internal one. I learned that this journey was less about success and more about confronting the inner insecurities that were I didn't know were holding me back.

I was never insecure about where I came from, because it's what made me. But I was insecure about knowing I could make it out of that life—crazy, right? Most people would be happy to have the brains, personality, and drive, and here I was scared to use everything I was gifted with, everything that got me out that first time so many years ago.

So before I was even able to make a move again, looking back I now realize God had me in a season where I was able to sit and reflect on my insecurities. I had to address the intersection between who I believed I was and who God said I was and be honest about what I needed in those moments. I knew it was now or never, and I knew my current situation was just a chapter helping me do the hard work to address everything that was keeping me from becoming.

So for a year straight I humbled myself before God. I sat at a desk in a hospital emergency room registering patients trusting God as He revealed His plans. I drove back and forth from Atlanta attending networking events. That's how I was able to build both my name and clientele in a city where I didn't even have an address yet. As I networked, I listened quietly to people's stories—but not necessarily to the tips they were offering.

It was kind of like eating the fish and spitting out the bones. I took what resonated and discarded the rest. I was listening for resilience and spoken fears with an urge for a better life, because that was me sitting in that crowd. It wasn't that I couldn't do it—I had already done it before; it was more that I needed a better understanding of my desires. But I also quickly learned that this question was something only I could answer: Why do I want to better my life, and how does bettering my life look to me? Everybody's definition of success is different. I never wanted to be rich in materials, but rich in ways that money cannot buy. A life filled with love, peace, health, time, freedom, and now purpose as I uncover the ways my gifts make room for me.

Resilience and Success as a Woman in Tech

Serena Sacks-Mandel

Ms. Sacks-Mandel is an international award-winning strategic visionary and sales and operations leader. She recently joined MGT as the field CTO supporting Social Impact Solutions and Technology Solutions Group. In her previous roles, she was the global chief technology officer at Microsoft for the education industry and the chief information officer at Fulton County Schools and Florida Virtual Schools. In both organizations she led the IT function to become "world-class," while enabling student-centric teaching and learning, which resulted in significant improvements in student outcomes.

Prior to pivoting to education, she led technology innovation teams at IBM, Walt Disney World, and Harcourt, Inc., and provided management consulting support for many other organizations. Ms. Sacks-Mandel has won numerous state, national, and global awards for her leadership, vision, technical excellence, and commitment to supporting women in technology. She recently published her book ***Empowered***: ***Frame your Narrative, Own your Power***.

Connect with Serena at www.SerenaSacksMandel.com.

———

When I decided to move to Atlanta and take on a challenging role as the chief information officer at Fulton County Schools, I had no idea what adventures awaited me. I was ready to leave behind my comfortable life in Orlando, Fla., where I had raised my two daughters and built a successful career in IT for over 20 years. I was eager to start a new chapter in a vibrant city, where I could make a positive difference for 100K students per year. Little did I know that I would face some of the toughest challenges of my life, both personally and professionally, and that I would have to slay some dragons along the way. But I also discovered that Atlanta is a city full of opportunities, support, and fun. And that with the right attitude, tools, and network, I could overcome any obstacle and achieve my goals. Here is my story of how I slayed Atlanta and built a rewarding and fulfilling life here.

One of the first things I had to deal with when I moved to Atlanta was the traffic. Oh, the traffic! If you have ever driven in Atlanta, you know what I mean. It is a nightmare of congestion, delays, and accidents. And I have a condition called "topographical disorientation," which means I get lost very easily, even with GPS. I can get lost in my own neighborhood or even in a parking lot. So you can imagine how stressful it was for me to navigate the busy streets and highways of Atlanta, especially when I was new to the city and had to find my way to work, meetings, and events. Luckily, I discovered the Waze app, which became my best friend and lifesaver. Waze not only gave me directions but also helped me avoid traffic jams, road closures, and speed traps. It also gave me some entertainment with its funny voices and comments. Without Waze, I would have probably ended up in Alabama or South Carolina by mistake, or spent hours stuck in traffic, cursing and crying.

Another challenge I faced was building a new professional network in a city where I didn't know anyone. I had left behind a strong network of colleagues, friends, and mentors in Orlando, and I had to start from scratch in Atlanta. But I was determined to make connections and establish myself as a leader in the tech community. So I did what any ambitious and sociable person would do: I went to every networking event I could find. On my first night in Atlanta, I attended a Women in Technology event, where I met some amazing ladies who welcomed me warmly and made me feel at home. They also gave me some tips and introductions that helped me get started in the Atlanta tech scene. From then on, I became a networking machine. I attended 4–6 events per week, sometimes two or three in one night. I met people from all walks of life, backgrounds, and industries. I learned a lot, shared a lot, and had a lot of fun. I also used LinkedIn and other social media platforms to keep in touch and build relationships. Within a few months, I had built a solid network of contacts, friends, and allies, who helped me grow my career and supported me in times of need.

But not everything was smooth sailing. I also had to deal with some personal hardships that tested my resilience and courage. I went through a painful divorce, which affected my relationship with my daughters. I had to support two homes, one in Orlando and one in Atlanta, which was costly and stressful. I had to travel back and forth to see my daughters, who were still living in Orlando with their father. Sometimes, I had to drop everything and drive seven hours to be with them, especially when one of them was going through some serious emotional issues. I also had to take care of my mother, who was diagnosed with Alzheimer's and had moved in with me after my stepfather passed away. All of this took a toll on me emotionally and physically, but I never gave up on my dreams. I kept working hard to improve the technology functions at Fulton County Schools and to make a positive impact on the students and staff. I also kept a positive outlook and a sense of humor, which helped me cope with the challenges and find joy in the small things.

As if that wasn't enough, I also had to fight a life-threatening disease. For two years, I battled a rare form of cancer, which required aggressive treatment and surgery. This was one of the scariest and most difficult experiences of my life, but I faced it with determination and optimism. I continued to work and fulfill my professional and nonprofit responsibilities, while undergoing treatment. I also continued to take care of my mother, who was losing her memory and needed constant attention. I was fortunate to have a great team of doctors, nurses, and caregivers who helped me through this ordeal. I was also blessed to have the support of my family, friends, and network who prayed for me, visited me, and encouraged me. I am happy to say that I beat cancer and I am now in remission. I am grateful for every day and every breath that I have.

Soon after I was cured, I met the love of my life. He is my soulmate, my partner, and my best friend. We are now happily married and enjoying life in Atlanta. This city has been good to me and has so much to offer. My oldest daughter is even planning to move here with her partner after she graduates with her MBA from Cornell Johnson Business School. I can't wait to welcome them and spoil my future grandkids!

Through all these trials and tribulations, I never lost sight of my purpose and my passion. I never let myself be a victim of circumstances. Instead, I used every challenge as an opportunity to learn, grow, and evolve. I also used every experience as a source of inspiration, wisdom, and compassion. I have learned so much from my journey, and I have gained so much from my adventures. I have also given back to the community and the world by sharing my story, mentoring others, and supporting causes that I care about. I have done things that I never imagined I would do like extreme skiing, global travel, and building a school for girls in Africa. I have lived a life full of challenges, but also full of rewards and fulfillment.

To sum up, my journey to Atlanta and my ability to overcome adversity is a story of slaying and success. I hope that my story inspires you to face your own challenges with courage and optimism, and to pursue your own dreams with passion and determination. I hope that my story also shows you that Atlanta is a great city in which to live, work, and play, and that with the right attitude, tools, and network, you can slay Atlanta too. My experiences and lessons learned along the way are valuable for anyone who wants to build a successful and fulfilling life, no matter where they are or what they do.

Beyond Bell's Palsy

Healing through the Pain

Dominique Serrano

Dominique Serrano, originally from Bronx, New York, is a lifestyle wellness coach, esthetician, and holistic healer with a passion for helping others achieve balance and wellness through mind, body, and skin connection. As the founder of Pure Divine Connection Beauty Wellness Studio, Dominique has created a sanctuary where beauty and wellness merge, offering transformative skincare therapies, detox treatments, and wellness services.

With a personal journey rooted in holistic healing, Dominique's approach to wellness deepened after her rapid recovery from Bell's palsy. Through juicing, meditation, high-alkaline foods, and self-care, she not only healed but also found inspiration to help others transform their lives. This led to the development of her signature programs, such as The 21-Day Mind Body Reset and the 7-Day Juice Reset & Detox, aimed at guiding clients through cleansing, rebalancing, and glowing from the inside out.

Dominique is also the visionary behind Pretty Girls Meditate (PGM), curating monthly events with movement designed to support women in their mental, emotional, and spiritual well-being. PGM focuses on meditation, sound healing, movement, and other holistic practices to help participants reduce stress, release trauma, and promote overall wellness. Through monthly events and the PGM SoulCare Retreat, Dominique provides women with the tools to cultivate self-care as a ritual and to heal and grow in a supportive community.

Her work, both as a coach and through Pure Divine Connection Beauty Wellness Studio, reflects her commitment to holistic health. Dominique emphasizes that beauty is more than skin deep—it's the connection between mind, body, and skin.

Website: www.dominiqueserrano.com
Instagram: https://www.instagram.com/domanetdivine

The Cocoon of Transformation

Imagine the pain a caterpillar endures as it transforms into a butterfly, cocooned in isolation, vulnerable to the unpredictable forces of the outside world—storms that rage, predators that lurk, and parasites that seek to weaken it. Yet, despite these challenges, the caterpillar perseveres, undergoing a profound metamorphosis. When the time comes to break free, it emerges transformed, ascending to new heights and viewing the world from an entirely different perspective.

My journey mirrors this transformation. Born and raised in the Bronx, New York, I've faced so much pain and trauma from a young age, much like the caterpillar weathering its trials. My life, marked by challenges from childhood through adulthood, was a testament to my resilience. Whether it was serving in the U.S. Air Force or battling personal struggles, I continually sought growth and healing.

But it was my diagnosis of Bell's palsy in 2022 that became the most defining chapter of my metamorphosis. Faced with the sudden paralysis of half my face, I entered my own cocoon—a period of intense self-reflection and healing. Through holistic practices like lifestyle wellness changes, setting boundaries, dietary changes, meditation, and sound healing, I began my ascent, overcoming what was supposed to be a prolonged recovery in just two and a half weeks.

Now, like the butterfly that has broken free, I see life from a new perspective. My journey through pain has elevated me to greater heights, inspiring others to embrace their own transformations with courage and hope.

Childhood and Early Trauma: The Birth of Resilience

My early life in the Bronx was shaped by both love and hardship. I grew up in a vibrant yet challenging environment. My parents separated and divorced when I was 11 years old, leaving me to navigate the complexities of a fractured family. The separation had a profound impact on me, creating a sense of instability and loss at a young age.

Amidst the challenges of growing up in a single-parent household, I endured experiences that left deep emotional scars. The trauma of molestation during my childhood introduced me to pain and confusion that no child should ever have to face. This experience, combined with the absence of a stable family structure, forced me to grow up quickly, developing a resilience that would carry me through the many trials of my life.

Despite the hardships, I found solace in the strong bonds I formed with friends and family members who supported me. These relationships provided me with a sense of belonging and security, even when the world around me seemed uncertain. However, the emotional weight of my early experiences lingered, shaping my sense of self-worth and influencing the choices I would make in the years to come.

As I grew older, I began to channel my pain into personal growth. Developing a fierce determination to overcome the obstacles in my path and refusal to be defined by the traumas of my past. This resilience, forged in the crucible of my early life, would become a defining characteristic of my journey, leading me to seek out opportunities for healing and transformation in the years that followed.

Adulthood and the Quest for Healing: The Struggles Intensify

As I transitioned into adulthood, my journey didn't get any easier. In 2005, I left New York City to serve in the U.S. Air Force—a decision that took me far from the Bronx and pushed me out of my comfort zone. My time in the Air Force introduced me to discipline and structure, and I formed bonds and friendships that remain strong to this day. But it also brought new challenges. I became a wife and mother, roles that added both joy and complexity to my life.

By 2008, I relocated to Atlanta, Ga., hoping for a fresh start. After graduating from college in 2011, I built a successful career as a photographer, capturing the beauty and stories of others even as I struggled with my own. Yet, beneath the surface, the unresolved pain from my past continued to fester. The strain of a failed marriage and separation from my son began to weigh heavily on me, affecting my overall well-being.

The burden of my past and present struggles began to take a toll on me as life continued to test me. In 2021, I faced the devastating loss of my home, the collapse of significant relationships, and a period of displacement that left me without a car or stable income. These compounded losses deepened the pain I had already endured, leaving me feeling isolated and vulnerable—much like a caterpillar cocooned in darkness, waiting for transformation.

The Diagnosis: Bell's Palsy and the Breaking Point

I knew I was carrying too much and needed to let it go. Crying is a powerful way to release what no longer serves you, and I allowed myself to do just that. But I didn't realize just how much pain I had been holding on to. That cry became a release for years of physical and emotional trauma I was holding on to. When it was over, I was left feeling completely drained, exhausted, and depleted. I knew then that it was time for a detox—my body just wasn't feeling right. Your body always tells you what it needs; you just have to listen and pay attention.

I woke up the next morning on July 2, 2022, with a terrible earache. I thought the overload from crying made this happen. The pain was so intense that I curled up in a ball for nearly four hours before it finally subsided, so I carried on with my day. Later that evening, I could feel something strange happening to my face. I didn't think much of it at first, but when I looked in the mirror, tears immediately streamed down my face. I was in disbelief, confused, and scared of my own reflection. My first thought was, "Am I having a stroke?"

Anyone's normal response would be to rush to the hospital, but not mine. After realizing it wasn't a stroke, I convinced myself that the best option was to just sleep it off. The next morning, I woke up to the harsh reality that this wasn't like the earache I had the day before—it wasn't just going to go away.

That's when I decided to use my AO Body Scan device, a tool I trust for detecting issues down to the cellular and DNA level. The scan revealed that my cranial nerves were inflamed. When I looked up what cranial nerves were associated with, Bell's palsy was the first thing that popped up. At that moment, I knew it was time to go to the hospital.

On July 3, 2022, I admitted myself to the hospital; I was officially diagnosed with Bell's palsy, a condition that causes sudden paralysis on one side of the face. For someone whose life had already been marked by so much pain, the diagnosis felt like the final blow in a series of relentless challenges. The paralysis was not just a physical affliction; it was a symbol of the emotional and psychological paralysis I had experienced throughout my life.

Doctors told me that my recovery could take anywhere from six months to a year, a prognosis that seemed to confirm my worst fears. The news was devastating. The woman who had spent years fighting to hold my life together was suddenly facing the possibility of a long and uncertain recovery. With the added fear that I might never smile the same way again. My face became a physical manifestation of the emotional battles I had been waging for years. It was a moment that could have easily broken my spirit and maybe a part of it did, but I chose to see it as an opportunity for profound change and transformation.

The Metamorphosis: Holistic Healing and Rebirth

Faced with the daunting challenge of recovery and prescriptions for various medications, I chose not to take them and instead decided to take control of my healing journey. I turned to holistic practices, convinced that true healing required addressing the mind-body-connection as a whole. This decision marked the beginning of my metamorphosis—a process of shedding old pain and embracing new growth and learning to trust my body's ability to heal itself. I began to meditate with sound healing daily, I tried acupuncture, I stretched daily and moved my body, and most importantly, I focused on my nutrition, all aimed at restoring balance to my body and mind. Each step deepened my understanding of the intricate connection between mental clarity and physical healing. As I embraced these holistic approaches, I began to feel more in tune with my body's needs. This commitment to natural healing became not only a path to recovery but also a way of life, one that empowered me to live with greater awareness and intention.

Committed to self-healing, I continued to focus on building habits that nurtured both my physical health and emotional well-being. Each day became a chance to push beyond my limits, not just physically, but mentally and emotionally as well. I learned to trust myself, to listen to my body, and to prioritize my well-being. I adjusted my diet to include nutrient-rich, anti-inflammatory foods, knowing that proper nutrition was essential for healing. I prioritized regular exercise, choosing activities that helped me regain my strength and mobility, while also relieving stress. Mindfulness became a daily practice. These lifestyle changes began to have a profound impact on my recovery.

Beginning with my diet, I adopted a regimen of juicing that helped to nourish my body from within. I saw the act of juicing as a metaphor for my own life—extracting the essential nutrients and discarding the toxins. Meditation was a practice that allowed me to confront my fear, quiet the chaos of my mind, and reconnect with my inner strength, allowing me to rediscover who I was.

Setting boundaries became another crucial aspect of my healing process. I realized that for me to truly heal, I needed to distance myself from the toxic relationships that had contributed to my stress and emotional pain. This period of self-imposed isolation, though difficult, was necessary for my transformation—much like the cocooning phase of a caterpillar.

Sound healing, a practice that uses vibrations to restore the body's natural balance, became another key element of my recovery. The soothing resonance of sound helped to calm my nervous system and support the healing of both my physical and emotional wounds. Through these holistic practices, I defied medical expectations, making a remarkable recovery in just two and a half weeks, and this girl was able to smile again.

The Emergence: A New Perspective on Life

My recovery from Bell's palsy marked the beginning of a new chapter in my life—a chapter defined by empowerment, self-love, and a renewed sense of purpose. Like the butterfly emerging from its cocoon, I broke free from the constraints of my past, embracing a new perspective on life. The pain and struggles I had endured, rather than breaking me, had become the foundation of my strength and resilience. I emerged from this period of healing with a new perspective on life. I faced my pain head-on, transforming it into a source of strength and inspiration.

With this newfound clarity, I decided to channel my experiences into helping others. I founded Pure Divine Connection Beauty Wellness Studio, a spa where beauty and well-being intertwine to kickstart a transformative journey of nurturing, relaxation, renewal, and rejuvenation for your mind, body, and skin. I also founded Pretty Girls Meditate, a sisterhood dedicated to healing and connection. Through these ventures, I have created a safe space for women to connect, heal, and grow—mirroring their own journey of transformation. Pretty Girls Meditate is a testament to my belief in the power of holistic healing and the importance of nurturing self-love and self-worth through meditation, music, movement, mindfulness, and nutrition.

Healing Through the Pain

My story is one of profound transformation. From a childhood overshadowed by trauma to an adulthood marked by challenges, I have always sought healing and growth. My diagnosis of Bell's palsy, though initially devastating, became the turning point for my most significant transformation yet. By embracing holistic practices, I was able to heal not only my physical body but also my spirit, emerging stronger and more resilient than ever before.

Today, I stand as a beacon of hope and inspiration for others who are navigating their own paths of pain and healing. My journey serves as a reminder that, like the caterpillar, we all have the power to transform our pain into strength, to break free from our cocoons, and to rise to new heights. Now, as a Holistic Wellness Healer, I use my experiences to guide others, helping them achieve their own growth through the power of self-care, resilience, and holistic healing.

Slaying in the City: My Journey from Colombia to Atlanta

Nathaly Tabares

Nathaly Tabares is a brand, commercial, and lifestyle photographer based in Atlanta, where she shares her life with her longtime love and their adorable new baby. Originally from Colombia, Nathaly's journey began with studies in aesthetics and nursing before she rediscovered her passion for photography. In 2017, she founded Nathaly Tabares Photography, dedicating herself to capturing unforgettable moments and empowering entrepreneurs to elevate their brands through impactful visuals.

More than just a photographer, Nathaly is a creative artist, fashion advisor, and enthusiastic cheerleader, committed to highlighting the unique essence of each client she works with. Her approach blends artistry with strategic planning and design, ensuring that every project reflects the client's authentic story.

Currently, Nathaly is working toward opening her own studio, envisioned not only as a space for her photography but also as a collaborative hub for other creators. With a vibrant spirit and a passion for serving her community and other Latinos, Nathaly is excited to continue her journey, inspiring others to shine while crafting visuals that resonate deeply.

https://www.instagram.com/nathalytabares.photography/
https://www.facebook.com/nathalytabares.photography
www.linkedin.com/in/nathaly-tabares-photography\
https://www.pinterest.com/nathalytabaresphotographyatl/
https://nathalytabaresphotography.com

———

Life has a way of throwing challenges at us, sometimes when we least expect it. Yet, those very challenges can carve out a path of empowerment, resilience, and celebration. My story begins in Cali, Colombia, where I was born in 1992. My childhood wasn't a fairy tale; it was filled with moments of scarcity and trauma. I experienced the weight of abuse, both toward my mother and myself. But through it all, I held onto a glimmer of hope. My spirit, resilient and unwavering, sought out the beauty in the world around me. Nature was my sanctuary, where I found joy in capturing the delicate dance of butterflies and the vibrant colors of flowers. Photography was not just a hobby; it was a seed planted in my heart long before I recognized its potential.

Despite the hardships, I pursued education fervently and earned my degrees in nursing and aesthetics. In Colombia, I became a nurse and an aesthetician, professions that allowed me to care for others and nurture their beauty. However, my life took a significant turn when I met the love of my life at the tender age of 15. He was living in Atlanta, also a Colombian. Our long-distance relationship, spanning six years, was fraught with challenges, yet it was also filled with dreams and hopes for a future together.

On November 30, 2014, I stepped off the plane in the United States, filled with aspirations and faith in a greater plan. Within weeks, I had my driver's license and was attending ESL classes while searching for jobs as a caregiver. My goal was to continue my career in aesthetics, but life had other plans. When the board of aesthetics denied my credentials, I felt as though my dreams had been shattered. But the fire within me refused to be extinguished. I had to pivot.

A chance conversation with an acquaintance opened a new door. She encouraged me to explore photography, suggesting I consider it as a side hustle. Without a moment's hesitation, I dove into online courses, eager to learn everything I could about this new craft. Nathaly Tabares Photography was born in 2017, alongside my work as a caregiver and, later, babysitter. I embraced every opportunity to snap photos, experimenting with various niches and pouring my heart into building a business that reflected my passion.

The journey wasn't easy. For the first three years, I didn't make any money, yet I invested in my dream—upgrading my website, purchasing camera equipment, and continuing my education in photography. There were countless moments when I wanted to throw in the towel, overwhelmed by doubt and fear. But I held onto my mantra: INSIST, PERSIST, AND NEVER DESIST! With my husband by my side, offering encouragement and perspective, I pushed through the darkest moments, trusting that God had a purpose for my journey.

My faith has been my anchor. The words from Joshua 1:9 have resonated deeply with me: "Have I not commanded you? Be strong and courageous. Do not be afraid; do not be discouraged, for the LORD your God will be with you wherever you go." I've embraced these words and sought to embody their message in my life.

As I navigated the growth of Nathaly Tabares Photography, I discovered my niche—branding photography. I began collaborating with entrepreneurs, thought leaders, and product brands, crafting visuals that resonated with their unique messages. The creative process transformed from a simple task into a collaborative celebration of identity and purpose. Each photoshoot became an opportunity to tell stories, inspire confidence, and elevate brands.

Last year marked a pivotal moment in my life. Not only did I rebrand my business, but I also welcomed my son, Luciano, into the world just two days before Christmas. He is my greatest blessing and serves as a constant reminder of the importance of perseverance. Motherhood has brought its own set of challenges, including the realities of postpartum depression, but it has also ignited an even deeper passion within me to build a legacy of hard work and entrepreneurial spirit.

I thrive on the joy of serving others and witnessing their excitement when they see their brand visuals. Atlanta, with its vibrant culture and Southern hospitality, has become my playground. I am particularly grateful to serve the Hispanic community, creating visuals that resonate with our shared experiences and backgrounds.

The journey has not been without its hurdles. As I look to the future, I envision opening a studio—an empowering space where I can serve my clients even better and foster a creative community for fellow creators. I am incredibly grateful to my husband for his unwavering support, to my clients for their trust, and to the mentors who have guided me along the way.

Every challenge has been an opportunity for growth, and every setback has paved the way for a comeback. I have learned that slaying in the city isn't just about personal success; it's about lifting others as you climb. When we embrace our journeys with open hearts, we create a ripple effect of empowerment that can inspire those around us.

So, to anyone reading this, remember: INSIST, PERSIST, AND NEVER DESIST. Work for your dreams and remain open to unexpected paths. Celebrate every small victory and learn from each stumble. Embrace your uniqueness and the power of your story. In the heart of Atlanta, we have a chance to make our mark, to slay in our own way, and to uplift others in the process.

Great things are on the horizon, and I'm excited for what lies ahead. Together, let's continue to create, inspire, and celebrate the journey, one beautiful moment at a time. Whether you're a fellow entrepreneur, a dreamer, or someone navigating the challenges of life, know that your story matters. Your journey is valid, and it has the potential to inspire others.

As we forge ahead, let's take a moment to acknowledge how far we've come. Each challenge faced, each fear conquered, and each dream pursued is a testament to our strength. In the spirit of celebration, let's lift our voices and share our stories, for they hold the power to illuminate paths for others.

Join me as we slay in the city, weaving our dreams into reality, and building a future filled with hope and possibility. Atlanta, here we come!

The Sweet Journey of Oh Sweet! Bakery: A Labor of Love, Family, and Flour

Sonya Vaverek

Sonya is the founder, owner, and head baker for Oh Sweet! Bakery. Baking has always been her passion—a way to de-stress at the end of the day, a way to show the people she loves that she loves them. Sonya is a firm believer that you must approach every batch in the right positive mind, otherwise the cupcakes will come out without the love necessary for them to taste oh so sweet!

Sonya has been baking since she could reach the counter, having learned from her mother and grandmother. She is self-taught, while raising her kids with her husband. Continuing to learn, serving others, and sharing sweet treats is her passion.

ohsweetbakery.com
FB: @Ohsweetbakerygoergia
IG: @ohsweetbakeryga

———

In the heart of Auburn, Georgia, sits a little gem known as Oh Sweet! Bakery. This boutique bakery was founded by the passionate and talented Sonya Vaverek in 2020—but its story doesn't begin with its official opening; the dream came long before, and was rooted in decades of love, dedication, and family traditions. Sonya's journey from being a child baking beside her mother to becoming a business owner is a testament to her enduring passion for baking, her love for family, and her commitment to making life's most special moments a little sweeter.

A Legacy Baked Into Every Loaf

For Sonya, baking isn't just a business—it's in her DNA. Raised in a home where the kitchen was always alive with the smells of freshly baked bread, cookies, and cakes, she quickly fell in love with the art of baking. "My mom baked every weekend," she recalls. "We always had homemade treats, and my parents even taught themselves to make gourmet chocolates, which we gave to friends during the holidays. My love for baking is truly genetic."

From a young age, Sonya watched her parents create culinary magic, and she quickly developed the same passion. The skills she learned at her mother's side became the foundation of her career, but her thirst for knowledge pushed her to continually refine and grow her craft.

The Road Less Traveled

After graduating from Florida State University, Sonya knew she wanted to pursue a career in pastry arts. However, life had other plans. She chose to follow her heart, moving to a new city to build a life with her soon-to-be husband. In the meantime, she kept her passion for baking alive through self-study. "I watched Martha Stewart and Julia Child religiously, and collected every baking cookbook I could find," she says. "I read them cover to cover and practiced constantly. When the internet came along, it opened up even more possibilities to learn and grow."

Sonya's love for baking never waned, even as she put her dream of attending culinary school on hold to raise her family. In fact, her passion only grew stronger as she continued to bake for family and friends, honing her core recipes and experimenting with new techniques.

A Turning Point: From Family Kitchen to Wedding Cakes

In 2012, Sonya experienced a turning point in her baking journey when she was asked to bake for her first wedding. "I was so excited!" she remembers. "My middle daughter, Emily, who was 12 at the time, was a huge help. She had taught herself to make sugar flowers and was really good at it!" Together, they worked on a tasting box and perfected the details for the wedding. The event was a resounding success, and Sonya was hooked on the idea of creating show-stopping cakes for life's most important moments.

That first wedding marked the beginning of Sonya's journey into professional baking. As her children grew older and more independent, Sonya felt the pull to finally pursue her dream in earnest.

Building a Dream During a Pandemic

When her youngest son became a senior in high school, Sonya knew it was time to focus on herself and her dream. "I'd put my career and dreams on hold to raise my family, which was the greatest joy of my life. But now that my kids were thriving, I felt it was time to pursue my passion for baking and owning a bakery."

Timing, as they say, is everything—and Sonya's dream of opening Oh Sweet! Bakery aligned with the onset of the global pandemic in 2020. Undeterred by the challenges of starting a business during such uncertain times, Sonya leaned on her family, friends, and deep faith. "With the support of my family and friends, and truly blessings from God, I was able to start my business and thrive," she says.

Oh Sweet! Bakery quickly adapted to the unique circumstances of the pandemic. Sonya began by offering deliveries and creating treat boxes that brought joy to people stuck at home. "We just baked, and we did what we could to make life a little sweeter during such a tough time."

A Mobile Bakery Named Lucille

In 2021, Sonya made a bold move that would set Oh Sweet! Bakery apart from the competition. She invested in a horse trailer that she lovingly named "Lucille" and converted it into a mobile bakery. "Lucille is the cutest little horse trailer, and now I take her to weddings, corporate events, school functions—anywhere people want to enjoy sweet treats on the go," Sonya explains.

The mobile bakery has been a huge hit, allowing Sonya to bring her delicious creations to a wider audience and serve her treats with a personal touch at events across the region. Lucille has become a signature part of the Oh Sweet! experience, adding charm and convenience to the business's offerings.

Constantly Growing and Learning

Since its humble beginnings in 2020, Oh Sweet! Bakery has grown beyond weddings and special events. Sonya has expanded her business into wholesale, providing delicious baked goods to local coffee shops and other businesses. But despite her success, she remains committed to learning and refining her skills. "I've had a lot to learn, especially when it comes to social media and marketing," Sonya admits. "It's been a fun challenge to grow my business, and I've had a lot of help from great people along the way."

Her dedication to her craft is evident in every cake, cookie, and pastry she creates. She is always exploring new techniques and developing innovative recipes to keep her customers coming back for more. "My goal for the future is to continue doing weddings and blessing people with sweets. I love seeing my brides come back for birthday cakes, baby shower treats, and other celebrations. It's such a joy to become a part of their lives and watch their families grow."

Giving Back to the Community

As Oh Sweet! Bakery continues to flourish, Sonya is committed to giving back to the community that has supported her journey. "We do a lot of community work, including donating baked goods to charities," she says. "God has blessed us in so many ways, and the only thing I can do is give back to others."

Sonya's generosity and passion for helping others are at the core of her business philosophy. She believes that success isn't just about creating delicious desserts—it's about making a positive impact on the lives of others, whether through a beautifully crafted wedding cake or a donation to a local charity.

Looking Ahead: Sweet Dreams for the Future

As Sonya looks to the future, she is filled with excitement and hope. "I hope my business continues to grow and flourish," she says. "My dream is that everyone will want an Oh Sweet! Bakery cake for their wedding and that we'll continue to be a part of people's celebrations for years to come."

With her unwavering dedication to quality ingredients, amazing taste, and personal connections, it's clear that Oh Sweet! Bakery is more than just a bakery—it's a labor of love that brings joy to every bite. From the homemade breads of her childhood to the wedding cakes she creates today, Sonya's passion for baking has shaped her life and touched the lives of countless others. And as her business grows, one thing is certain: the future looks oh-so-sweet.

Slaying in Atlanta: Molding the Life I Want

Molly Sanyour

Molly Sanyour is a dynamic ceramics artist, entrepreneur, and educator whose journey is as vibrant as her creations. Known for her boundless energy and positivity, Molly's love for clay has taken her around the world, learning and taking classes from renowned potters. Her entrepreneurial spirit shines through Molly Sanyour Ceramics, where she crafts unique and captivating pieces. With a knack for teaching, Molly has inspired countless students through her engaging and innovative ceramics classes. Always documenting her adventures with her Meta glasses and selfie stick, Molly is now on the exciting path to opening her own studio in Atlanta, embracing full-time entrepreneurship and inspiring others to follow their dreams.

www.mollysanyourceramics.com
Tiktok/Instagram/Facebook/YouTube/SkillShare: @mollysanyourceramics

———

Do you ever think of your 80-year-old self and try to live each day of your life making her proud, creating a life for her to be excited to recount? What about your eight-year-old self? Do you ever think back to her dreams? Are you brave, bold, and making her proud? I think about those versions of myself all the time; they are what drove me to uproot my life a year ago in pursuit of my dreams. This is my story.

I was born and raised in Richmond, Va. My parents were high school sweethearts and are still married; I am the youngest of three girls. Our family is really tight-knit, which makes sense, considering we grew up sharing one bathroom! Every member of my family has played a role in where I am today. My dad is Lebanese and comes from a family of entrepreneurs in the food industry. My mom juggled staying home and working. She always infused creativity into everything around us—from finding old furniture to paint in various designs, to painting funky colors on our walls at home, to running her own monogramming business.

When we look back on our childhoods, there are often clues that show us signs of what we dreamed of becoming. I have memories of playing "business" with my sisters. We would write up receipts, exchange "money," and pass handwritten documents through the slats of a chair. My dad would even let us play with the cash register from his family's old restaurant, which made it feel real!

At school growing up, each year we would create a figure out of clay on the holidays. Over the years, we had quite an accumulation. Most students had created four or five pieces by graduation; I, on the other hand, having found pockets of time to sneak to the art room for extra creating, had 20! Looking back, this time of my life was a seed planting my love of art and business.

Despite this love of art, by high school, art was low on my priority list. At one point I was advised to drop my art elective to take extra math or science classes so I could get into a "good" college. At that time, I was more into sports and friends than art, and let's be real—society, or at least the society I grew up in, never represented art as a successful career path. After graduation, I found myself at James Madison University, where I dabbled in various majors. At the time, I wasn't sure if I wanted to be a lawyer or pursue business school, but the reality of the rigor of the economics and statistics course loads led me to change course.

Meanwhile, I joined the girls' club lacrosse team and learned more about the possibilities and opportunities for art majors. One of my teammates was there on a photography scholarship, which opened my eyes to ceramics. I found myself thinking of the saying, *If you do what you love, you never work a day in your life.* And I thought, "This is it." I remember calling my mom as I walked across campus on my way home from my first art elective to let her know I had found my new major—ceramics! Her response was perfect. Not only was she excited for me, but she also encouraged me to get my teaching degree to offer some stability to my future. My inner eight-year-old self was bursting thinking about the possibility of having a career as an art teacher!

Entering the workforce, I was so excited and nervous. I was told that finding a job as an art teacher would be difficult unless someone retired or went on leave. However, I was offered a job after my first interview—an art teacher position at a K-5 Title 1 elementary school just down the road from my house. Talk about too good to be true! During this time, I realized how lucky I was to have had access to a ceramics studio in college, and I continued to pursue my ceramics passion by taking classes at community studios while teaching full-time.

After eight years in that position, my dream job opened up at my former high school, which had recently unveiled a new arts facility. The ceramics studio was one that I had never seen before. It offered a wheel for every student, endless supplies, and plenty of room to create as a community. I really felt like I had reached my dreams. During this time, I built a home studio and opened my business, Molly Sanyour Ceramics, to supplement my teaching salary. As I continued to create in my home studio and teach students the foundations of clay, my social media and my business grew—from brand deals to sponsorships to having ceramic tools created with my name on them. The peak was when I made a butt mug for Lizzo, which she made famous through a Dove campaign and a Vogue interview, leading to a successful Kickstarter to mass-produce my butt mugs. Molly Sanyour Ceramics was on top of the world!

Then COVID hit. It was during COVID that my eyes were opened to the racial injustices our country faces and the flaws in our education system. I had been at my job, growing the ceramics program, growing my social media, teaching workshops across the country, and having my work sold in the Virginia Museum of Fine Arts. As I tried to use my voice for good, I quickly realized that speaking out against institutional racism gets a scarlet letter drawn on your chest. My dream job had lost its luster, and I had to reflect on what I wanted from this one life. What would my 80-year-old self have to say about me staying in a position that no longer served me?

I knew I had to make a jump and make a change, but actually doing it was way harder than I ever imagined. I kept leaning on the excitement I would have for my future self if I made the change—if I quit my job, made a move, and molded my life into this dream I had envisioned, opening a pottery studio where I could be in control of the culture, the schedule, and the community.

People often ask why I chose Atlanta. My answer? My boyfriend. He was from Atlanta, and in the animation industry, some say that Atlanta is the Hollywood of the South. He saw my potential in ceramics and my desire to become the Martha Stewart of Clay. His push, along with turning 40 and trying to live a life I'd be excited to recount (which I credit in part to having two older sisters whose advice and insight would fuel most of my bravest decisions) led me to finally make the plunge. I quit my job and moved to Atlanta with the goal of opening a studio. I didn't know anyone in Atlanta and had only visited on brief trips with my boyfriend.

My Atlanta community quickly grew; I had gained over 100,000 followers on Instagram over the years through sharing my clay journey. Soon the internet started connecting me to wonderful, welcoming clay people in Atlanta! I would enthusiastically meet up for lunches and coffees with anyone who invited me.

Arriving in Atlanta, in June 2023, I hit the ground running. A quick Google search on how to find money to open a business led me to apply for a low-interest business loan through Invest Atlanta. I also walked every day, trying to find a studio within walking distance of our home, because if you know Atlanta, the traffic is thick! The first place I fell in love with fell through—literally, the floors were too weak to support the pottery equipment. I connected with contractors and architects, went through multiple spaces, and faced months of trying to lock down a lease and funding. Eventually, things came together. In February 2024, I found a new construction space, by June 2024 I was finally approved for the loan and by July, I sold my house in Richmond and used the capital to start the business. This chapter has been both terrifying and exhilarating.

Now, each day, I'm bringing Molly Sanyour Ceramics Studio to life. My mission is to create a studio that is a Clay Paradise. We have multi-week classes, workshops, a creative community, and ample equipment—from clay beginners to seasoned sculptors, all ages and talents are welcome. (I'm basically building Hogwarts for potters.)

The future's bright, and I'm grateful to be starting off here in Atlanta. It already feels like home! I hope to inspire and encourage you to spend time reflecting back on the signs from your own childhood as you look ahead and create the life you want to mold for yourself! Be bold, take risks, and make your 80-year-old self excited to recount your stories!

About the Curator, Leigh M. Clark

Four-time best-selling author Leigh M. Clark is known for her inspiring books, including *The Dream is in Your Hands*, *Living Kindly*, and the *Slay the USA* series. Her work as an author has empowered and motivated countless readers by highlighting kindness, resilience, and the strength of community. In addition to her writing career, Leigh has over 20 years of experience as a business strategist, working with Fortune 500 companies to help them grow and succeed.

Leigh's latest project, the Slay the USA series, is a growing national movement that shines a spotlight on extraordinary women across the country who are leaving their mark on their communities and industries. Through this series, Leigh is empowering these women to share their stories of triumph, leadership, and impact, much like she has done in her own life. The series is rapidly expanding, highlighting women in cities from coast to coast, celebrating their contributions and inspiring others to follow their lead.

Leigh's expertise and passion for leadership and empowerment have made her a sought-after speaker, with multiple appearances on the TEDx stage. Her stories of kindness and personal growth have been featured in prominent publications like *HuffPost* and shared through appearances on *The Today Show* and the *Rachael Ray Show*.

As the founder of Kindleigh, a movement focused on giving back through acts of kindness, Leigh has led initiatives that have raised significant funds for charitable causes. Her mission is to create lasting change through kindness and sharing stories of impact, further solidifying her role as a leader in philanthropy.

Leigh resides in Southwest Florida with her son, Carter, and the love of her life. She's here to make an impact and leave her mark by illuminating others.

"Don't let the world change your heart. Let your heart change the world." - Leigh M. Clark

IG:@leighmclark @slaytheusa

www.leighmclark.com

www.slaytheusa.com

Milton Keynes UK
Ingram Content Group UK Ltd.
UKHW021126021124
450589UK00014B/1271

9 781958 481387